Shape your body shape your life

Shape your body shape your life

THE WEIGHT TRAINING WAY TO TOTAL FITNESS

TONY LYCHOLAT

Patrick Stephens
Wellingborough, Northamptonshire

First published 1987

British Library Cataloguing in Publication Data

Lycholat, Tony
Shape your body, shape your life.
1. Weight lifting
I. Title
796.4'1   GV546.5

ISBN 0-85059-869-9

Patrick Stephens Limited is part of the Thorsons Publishing Group

Printed and bound in Great Britain

Contents

Acknowledgements

A book reflects the work of many people, not just the author. Many thanks must go to all my past students who asked so many of the questions which are hopefully answered here; to Atlanta Sports Industries, Richard Winstanley and Sandra Bradley for their generosity and help with the filming of the exercises; to Julie Davies for being a patient model; to all my friends who put up with the irritability which always accompanies my writing; to my publishers, Patrick Stephens Ltd, for putting this book together; and most of all, thanks to Rene Randerson who listened to me in the kitchen.

Introduction

Why exercise?

People who exercise regularly look different from those who do not. Someone who has been following a well-designed and appropriate exercise programme will usually have well-shaped limbs, tall and erect posture, a firm abdomen and will move with a certain ease.

If you were to carry out a number of standard tests, the average exercising member of the public would also have greater muscular strength and endurance, more stamina, greater aerobic fitness, less body fat, and a wider range of movement than the average non-exercising member of the public. The exerciser, because of his/her greater strength and mobility would also have stronger and more injury resistant joints. His/her body systems would be generally more efficient, such that the individual's ability to carry out daily tasks would be improved, leaving more energy available to do other things. It is likely that the exerciser would also sleep better and that the regular exercise would also leave him/her with a reduced risk of coronary heart disease, and any tendency to become obese.

Research into how the human body responds to exercise also indicates that regular physical activity can be used to help in the clinical management of diabetes and high blood pressure, as well as preventing a deterioration of bone mass (osteoporosis) which commonly occurs as a result of ageing and inactivity. Some studies have also found evidence to indicate that regular exercisers are less susceptible to minor illnesses such as colds and 'flu — although this is far from conclusive. There also seems to be a link between other 'healthy' patterns of life and regular exercise: people who exercise regularly also tend to abuse their bodies less, by not smoking or eating high fat foods for example.

These are the positive physical effects of exercise. Yet more and more researchers are now concentrating upon the psychological effects of exercise, for several very good reasons. If you ask a person who exercises regularly a few questions, they would probably tell you that they felt better as a result of their physical activity. Not only that, but they would probably also go on to say that they were now more confident and more self assured, which allowed them to approach their life in a more positive way.

Why someone should feel better as a result of exercising has several explanations. Fairly recently it was discovered that the body was capable of releasing various hormones into the bloodstream which not only make you feel good, but were also capable of acting in a similar way to painkillers. It has been suggested that it is the presence of these circulating hormones released during strenuous exercise which are responsible for the feeling of exercise elation now commonly referred to as 'Runners High'.

Yet there are other, perhaps more accurate explanations too, especially since it would appear that the level of circulating hormones are probably too low in the majority of recreational exercisers to create the immense feelings of satisfaction and well being which many exercisers regularly report.

For a long time it has been known that how a person feels depends upon many factors, not least how they see themselves from the point of body image and self esteem. With exercise now being a very socially acceptable thing to do, people who take up exercise will perhaps be feeling better in the first instance, precisely because they will be engaging in an activity which is approved of by friends, neighbours and work colleagues. Couple this too, with the sense of satisfaction anyone gets from starting something and finishing it — an exercise session or a run for example. Add this to the fact that you know from the things you have read that exercising is 'good for you'. Take all these positive feelings now and add them to a body, which as a result of regular and appropriate exercise, is changing shape: a body which is assuming the characteristics of the regular exerciser as described at the beginning of the chapter and it is small wonder that you will feel psychologically better too.

Without doubt, the changes in physical appearance which occur as a result of systematic exercise and physical activity lead to a change in body shape which manifests itself as a change in the way a person sees themselves; a change in self/ body image. Body image is tied up in a complex way to self esteem. More and more researchers are showing that when you feel good about your body, you tend to feel good about your self, and when you feel good about your self, you will behave in a lively, energetic and more positive way.

The many studies which have investigated the relationship between exercise and mental health increasingly show that exercise can be used to improve the way a person feels, enabling them to act both more confidently and assertively. As a result, exercise is being used more and more to manage the symptoms of stress and depression — with considerable success. Shape your body, shape your life, in fact.

1

Why weight training?

This is a book about exercise, and in particular a book about exercising with weights. Why choose weight training as the activity upon which to base an exercise programme? Many people ask this question, usually because they have confused weight training with weight lifting. Weight lifting, as exemplified in Olympic competition is all about lifting the heaviest possible weight above your head. Such an activity is highly specialized, and whilst fascinating in terms of human achievement, appeals to none but a very few when it comes to taking up the sport. Weight lifters train with weights, but in a very specific way. Similarly the extremely muscular Mr Universe types also train with weights, but their training regime is aimed at gaining maximum size and symmetry, an aim which again requires highly specialized weight training and a certain type of body in the first place.

This book is not about extremes, nor is it about immensely complicated and demanding training programmes. Quite simply, this book is for the average person who wants to improve his or her shape, physical appearance, fitness and health through weight training. Using weights can help everyone to do this, since the results you get from weight training are largely dependent upon how you use those weights and what type of exercise programme you follow. More and more people are now taking up weight training and realizing that they can, in a short period of time achieve quite dramatic results in terms of how they look and feel. Unlike other activities, weight training allows you to work all parts of the body through a full range. Weights can also be used to improve fitness on several levels, as will be seen in a later chapter. Weight training is easy, and monitoring your progress is simple and satisfying.

If you really want to shape your body and see results which will lead you to approach life in an altogether different way, then exercising with weights cannot be bettered.

Many people have been put off the idea of weight training because of myths and old wives tales. For instance, it is not true that training with weights leads to huge bulging muscles. Massive increases in muscular size do not occur unless you have the right body type in the first place, follow a highly intensive training regime for several hours each day and accompany this training with huge intakes of food.

Women tend *not* to increase the size of their muscles to Herculean proportions since their hormonal balance is different from that of men. The average female has a much lower level of the male hormone testosterone, which is responsible for much of the tissue building effect in the body. This does not mean that weight training for women is useless — quite the contrary. Numerous studies indicate that women can increase their strength dramatically without a corresponding massive increase in size. Practically, this means a firmer muscle, which along with the other effects of training lead to a leaner and more shapely body.

Many people fear becoming 'muscle bound' as a result of weight training. A well designed and implemented training programme does not lead in any way to a loss of flexibility — in fact the opposite is the case, with many regular weight trainees exhibiting a remarkable range of movement.

Muscle soreness is another worry. As with any exercise programme, undue muscle soreness, particularly that which occurs one or two days after the exercise session (delayed onset muscle soreness) is invariably the result of doing too much exercise too soon. If you follow the guidelines in this book, this will seldom, if ever, be a problem.

2
Components of fitness

It could be that you want to be 'fitter' — whatever that means. It could be that you would like a better shape. It could be that you would like better posture, or to go about your life without feeling exhausted. The potential total benefits of exercise are numerous. Yet not all of the benefits of exercise listed in the first chapter occur with any and every type of exercise. Increased fitness and improved shape come as a result of doing different types of exercise in different ways for different components of fitness.

These days the idea of the four 'S' words, namely Stamina, Strength, Suppleness and Skill, representing fitness has been ousted by the concept of fitness which includes health-related and skill-related components. The health-related components of fitness are those which if improved, lead to an improvement in the general health of the person. Briefly, they are:

1. Cardiorespiratory efficiency (or how good you are at supplying fuel for activity and eliminating and dispersing those products which cause fatigue).
2. Muscular endurance (or the ability of a muscle or group of muscles to repeatedly perform exercise without fatigue).
3. Strength (or the ability of a muscle or muscle group to exert maximum force).
4. Flexibility (which indicates the range of movement which you possess at your joints).

Components of Physical Fitness.

Physical Fitness

'Health Related' Fitness
- Cardio-Respiratory Endurance
- Muscular Endurance
- Muscular Strength
- Flexibility
- Body Composition

'Skill Related' Fitness
- Agility
- Balance
- Co-Ordination
- Speed
- Power
- Reaction Time

5. Body composition (which reflects how much fat and how much lean tissue (muscle, bone, etc.) a person has).

The skill-related components are those which enable you to perform activities or movements patterns more efficiently. These are self explanatory in definition and include: agility; balance; speed; co-ordination; power; reaction time.

This book is not about developing sports and skill-related activities. Rather the emphasis of this book is on developing fitness and modifying your shape through exercises and training. As they are defined, the health-related components of fitness do not mean that much. Breaking them down in terms of noticeable benefits to you, is far more beneficial in terms of deciding what you need to do to get the results that you want.

COMPONENTS OF FITNESS — *what they mean to you in terms of fitness, health and shape*

1. Cardiorespiratory efficiency

An increase in the efficiency of this system means that you will find it easier to carry out all those activities which rely heavily upon the 'heart and lungs'. You will often find that this component is referred to along with muscular endurance as 'aerobic fitness'. Improving your aerobic fitness has been the aim of virtually all exercise programmes and the subject of many popular books, most notably those of Dr Kenneth Cooper, with very good reason.

Increased aerobic fitness has been linked very strongly with a reduction in an individual's risk of coronary heart disease — a decrease in high blood pressure. Aerobic exercise programmes have been used with considerable success in the management of obesity, diabetes, and clinical depression. Circulating levels of dangerous fats in the bloodstream have been seen to be reduced as a result of regular aerobic exercise, and prolonged aerobic exercise such as running for an hour or more does lead to a sense of euphoria brought about by increased levels of circulating hormones (endorphins).

If the aerobic exercise in question subjects joints to some form of mechanical stress, such as running does, those joints which are stressed will become stronger and more injury resistant. Aerobic exercise is also that which has been studied most with regard to positive mood states and feelings of well being, linked to more positive and less anxious behaviour.

The sum of the changes associated with aerobic exercise also means that any aerobic activity becomes less demanding — in other words you do not have to work as hard in order to do it. As your leisure pursuits are now physically less demanding, you will have more energy left for other activities that you want to do, than you had previously. Being able to do the things you want to do, as opposed to the things you have to do is very important when it comes to living life to the full.

In terms of your shape, aerobic exercise, if carried out systematically, and if it is of sufficient intensity, can use substantial amounts of stored body fat as fuel for exercise. This means that you can actively decrease your percentage of body fat with an appropriate exercise programme. If you have only a few pounds to lose it is often possible to keep your diet more or less as it is, and use exercise alone to achieve the required weight loss — and because you are exercising you can guarantee that this weight loss is all fat, and not water or muscle, as it the case with many 'semi-starvation' diets. If you have a considerable amount of fat weight to lose, then a combination of a diet, and aerobic exercise is the best method to follow.

Obviously, decreasing your body fat in some way, is going to make your body shaplier — since it is the fat under your skin which gives a rounded (or very rounded!) appearance. When the extra, unnecessary fat has gone, your muscles, which as a result of the regular exercise have become firmer, can show through.

It is important to realize however, that not all body fat is unnecessary, and that some is essential for vital body processes. Losing too much body fat can be hazardous to health, and not only are the amounts for men and women different, different types of bodies seem to be able to lose or gain body fat more readily than others. Essential fat, and body types are dealt with in the next section on assessing your body and setting your goals.

Traditional aerobic exercise (such as running, cycling, etc) does have its drawbacks in terms of the overall benefits which it offers. Whilst cardiorespiratory efficiency can be improved if you follow the appropriate guidelines, your muscular endurance will only be improved in those muscles which are being used repeatedly — such exercise is in many ways very specific. If you are following a running or cycling programme, for instance, only the muscles involved in running or cycling, those of the legs and buttocks

predominately, will improve in their endurance. Muscles of the upper body will remain very much in the same condition as they were before you started the exercise programme. Conditioning and shaping the upper body requires that upper body exercise of a certain type, frequency and duration must also be carried out if you are to get equal benefits in terms of fitness and shape in the upper and lower body.

2. Muscular endurance and
3. Muscular Strength

Muscular endurance is often confused with muscular strength. Muscular endurance enables a muscle or muscle group to repeatedly carry out work, to perform exercise, without getting tired. Muscular strength, on the other hand tells you how much force that muscle can exert — how much you can lift or carry, for instance. Muscular strength is short term and involves maximal amounts of force: muscular endurance is long term, and involves less than maximal amounts of force which are repeated often.

A person is strong if they can lift heavy weights, whilst the person who has muscular endurance can repeatedly lift that weight up and down without getting tired.

It is possible, and normal to have at the same time muscles which are very strong, and muscles which possess considerable amounts of endurance throughout the body. Muscular endurance permits you to perform tasks repeatedly in daily life without becoming over-tired — leaving you with more energy to enjoy yourself. Strong muscles do not just mean you can lift heavy weights — they also mean that if your limbs are subjected to sudden, abnormal forces, your muscles can help in protecting and stabilizing your joints. Possessing both muscular strength and endurance is important in maintaining erect and appropriate posture, whether you are standing, sitting, or moving.

A muscle's strength or endurance is greatly influenced by the work or exercise you ask it to do. Muscles which are unused tend to become soft and yielding to the touch, and have little shape and definition. Increasing the general muscular endurance of all your major muscle groups leads to firmer and more defined muscles — often without any increase in size. Exercising for muscular strength leads to stronger, firmer muscles, which, depending upon how you exercise and your body type, may also be accompanied by an increase in size.

4. Flexibility

Being flexible enables you to reach, bend and twist with ease. It means you can carry out all your necessary tasks and expend less energy doing so — a body which has a wide range of movement is one which can often take full benefit of its movement potential. Incorrect posture can be caused not only by weak muscles, but also by having a decreased range of movement at a joint or within muscles — improving your flexibility can lead to more appropriate and correct posture, whether you are walking standing or sitting.

Most exercise programmes tend to neglect this health-related component of fitness such that individuals often lack a good range of movement and are sometimes left with 'bulky' looking limbs and musculature. As part of an exercise programme, work on improving flexibility can help considerably when it comes to avoiding injury and relieving muscle soreness, should you get carried away in your enthusiasm to get results!

5. Body composition

Your weight actually says very little about you, since all it tells you is what everything, lumped together, weighs. It would be more useful to know what percentage of your body is fat-free and what percentage of your body is fat weight, since it is the fat weight which in excess, is hazardous to health, does not contribute to fitness and leaves you with a very rounded and flabby appearance if you are carrying too much of it.

Normally, the average healthy male has a body fat percentage of some 15-20 per cent of his total body weight, with the average female having some 25-30 per cent of her total weight. The differences in percentage body fat between males and females is sex specific and seems to relate to child rearing functions. Obesity in the male is characterized by a percentage of body fat greater than 20 and in the female by a percentage greater than 30.

You can also have too little fat, and health problems arise when the percentage of body fat drops to around 4 and 12 per cent in males and females respectively. People who exercise a lot, especially endurance athletes are often very close to these minimal figures.

Changing body composition through exercise is possible in two main ways. As we saw with aerobic exercise, fat can be used as fuel for the exercise provided the guidelines are followed. Exercise, if it is of a type which leads to the building of muscle, can also change body composition by increasing the fat-free weight, since muscle makes up a large proportion of the fat-free weight of the body.

HOW YOUR BODY 'SEES' EXERCISE

With all the positive benefits of exercise that we have discussed so far, in terms of both physical and psychological changes, it is easy to see why many people are regular exercisers, yet how can the many and varied positive effects of exercise be reconciled with the reported instances of injury and even death which we see in the newspapers? How can something which would seem to be so beneficial cause so many reported casualties? Truthfully, anybody who suddenly starts exercising after a period of inactivity is putting themselves at risk. Your personal 'risk factor' is going to depend upon many variables which will be discussed below.

Note that in talking about the benefits of exercise, a number of key words have cropped up: regular; progressive; systematic; appropriate. Such words indicate something about the nature of exercise; that it must follow some pattern — rules as it were, and it must be suited to you, the individual, in the first place. An exercise programme needs a design, a certain logic, which must take the exerciser as the starting point initially, and the exerciser must always be the point of reference throughout the programme.

All the instances of injury reported in the press, real or exaggerated, have common features, and are almost entirely avoidable. The fact that they occurred at all reflects not that the person was exercising, was injured and exercise is bad for you, as many critics claim, but that the person injured was doing an exercise activity *which was not suitable for him/her*

at the time.

Your exercise regime needs to be appropriate at all times. Making an exercise programme appropriate, getting the benefits you want, and avoiding the injuries you have read about is fairly simple, but it is useful to know how your body responds to exercise.

The fact that we continue to live day after day, reflects that unique trait of all organisms to survive. A complex organism, like ourselves, survives by constantly monitoring what is going on, not only in its external environment, but also by keeping a close watch upon what is going on in its internal environment.

By doing this, and knowing with considerable accuracy what is happening in and around it, the human body can react very quickly and effectively to any changes which may be hazardous. For example, if the temperature of the body rises unacceptably, we do something about it — our bodies can sweat, thereby losing heat by evaporation. Such an adaptation is immediate, and takes place precisely because such an increase in temperature could threaten the survival of the body.

It is as if the body has a set of normal values which represent a safe internal environment — a body which is not under threat and can survive quite happily. If changes occur which lead to a change in any of the variables being monitored within the internal environment, the body adapts accordingly to restore the balance.

Ask your body to do some physical

activity, and a whole host of changes occur within the body which require some form of adaptation, depending upon the activity you ask it to do.

Start running for example, and suddenly your body will have to start directing blood to the working muscles in large volumes, so that oxygen and nutrients can be used by the muscles to provide energy for the work you are now doing. A whole range of adaptations are suddenly required involving not only the heart, blood, blood vessels, lungs, musculature, nervous system etc. but all sorts of systems and mechanisms. In fact the whole body responds with an attempt to keep the internal environment of the body stable, and safe.

How well the body does this is going to depend not only upon the work you have asked your body to do, but also upon what else your body may be having to do at the same time (fighting disease for example, or recovering from injury), and how efficient and tuned up your body is for the activity in question. If the body becomes overloaded excessively by what it is doing, injury and nausea are common results. If there are certain structural defects in any of your body's systems or components, (heart for example) and you ask your body to engage in sudden strenuous activity, sudden death is possible.

If however, you repeatedly ask your body and its systems to do more work than normal, but not enough to cause *distress*, a number of changes will occur: adaptations designed to make the body better able to cope with the work you have asked it to do, will be made. Your body and it's systems will effectively undergo changes which make them more efficient — you become 'fitter'.

This 'Stress Theory' of exercise is summarized in the following diagrams. Here it can be seen that many factors can affect what is going on in the body, ranging from what your present health is like to how you feel, as well as less obvious ones perhaps, like your current worries, relationships and responsibilities. All of these factors need to be taken into account in some way, since how they affect your body is going to reflect how your body responds to an exercise programme.

In other words, your exercise programme must begin with an assessment of you. And in assessing you, care needs to be taken such that any programme designed for you is realistic (ie, the goals can be achieved by you). Once this has been done, the exercise programme can be designed bearing in mind the important elements which add up to make the training 'stimulus', namely, the type of exercise; the intensity of that exercise, how long that exercise lasts, and how often that exercise needs to be repeated for maximum benefit.

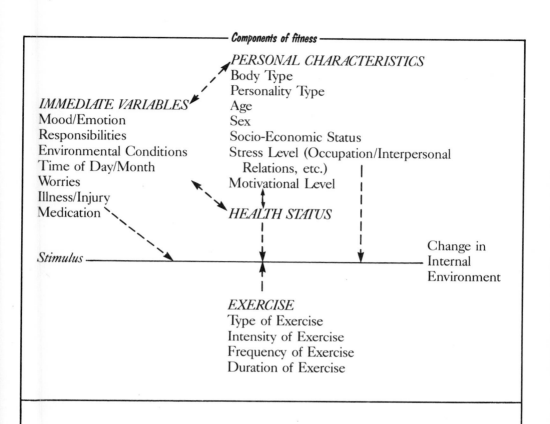

PERSONAL CHARACTERISTICS
Body Type
Personality Type
Age
Sex
Socio-Economic Status
Stress Level (Occupation/Interpersonal
    Relations, etc.)
Motivational Level

IMMEDIATE VARIABLES
Mood/Emotion
Responsibilities
Environmental Conditions
Time of Day/Month
Worries
Illness/Injury
Medication

HEALTH STATUS

Stimulus

Change in
Internal
Environment

EXERCISE
Type of Exercise
Intensity of Exercise
Frequency of Exercise
Duration of Exercise

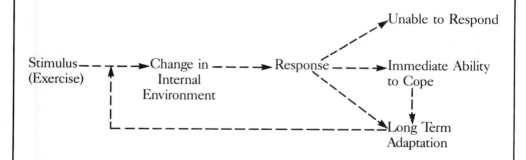

Stimulus
(Exercise)

Change in
Internal
Environment

Response

Unable to Respond

Immediate Ability
to Cope

Long Term
Adaptation

Diagrams to summarize the stress theory of exercise

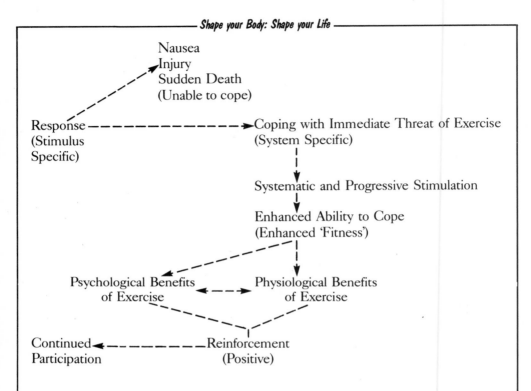

Nausea
Injury
Sudden Death
(Unable to cope)

Response ————————————→ Coping with Immediate Threat of Exercise
(Stimulus   (System Specific)
Specific)

Systematic and Progressive Stimulation

Enhanced Ability to Cope
(Enhanced 'Fitness')

Psychological Benefits   Physiological Benefits
of Exercise   of Exercise

Continued ← — — — — — — Reinforcement
Participation   (Positive)

The body's 'vision' of exercise summarized in diagrammatic form

3

Assessing yourself:

Are you fit to exercise?

The vast majority of people are fit to begin exercising without taking any precautions, other than making sure that they are embarking on a well-designed and appropriate exercise programme. Yet there are some people who would be wise to consult further and seek more specialist advice from their GP and/or an exercise specialist. This is particularly so if you can answer yes to the following questions:

1. Has your doctor ever told you that you have high blood pressure, or any cardio-vascular problem?
2. Is there any history of heart disease in your family?
3. Have you ever been troubled by unaccountable chest pain or tightness in the chest, especially if associated with minimal effort?
4. Are you prone to headaches, fainting or dizziness?
5. Have you any medical condition which you think might interfere with your participation in an exercise programme?
6. Do you suffer from pain or limited movement in any joint?
7. Are you taking any drugs or medication at the moment?
8. Are you extremely overweight or extremely underweight?
9. Are you a newcomer to exercise and over 40?
10. Are you pregnant?

If you are aware of your present health status, by the fact that you have regular health checks, so much the better, particularly if you rarely take part in any form of physical activity, either recreational or competitive, and if your job entails sitting down for most of the day. Asking yourself a few simple questions now, before you even being an exercise programme, and getting advice if you are at all unsure about your fitness to participate in any exercise activity is well worth the few minutes it takes.

HONEST SELF ASSESSMENT

The benefits of exercise have now been outlined in some detail — by now you are probably quite sure what you want and need from an exercise programme. For the majority of people, a combination of the benefits which have been outlined under each component of fitness is probably what is required. Some people may feel that they need to do more exercise with a very specific aim in mind, like changing body composition drastically, for example. But are you right in your assessment in the first instance, and are you being truthful with yourself? How much work do you really have to do, and are your expectations realistic?

There are several different ways of assessing your initial condition, some of which involve very specialized and extremely sensitive equipment, which in the right hands can give you a very accurate appraisal of your current health and fitness status.

If you have already gone through the simple questionnaire in the previous section, you will know that you are healthy enough to begin an exercise programme. What you will not know is exactly how healthy — more detailed information about how well your body is working can be provided by getting a thorough check up with your doctor, or at one of the many private health assessment centres up and down the country. Most of these centres, and virtually all fitness and health clubs nowadays, will give you some form of 'fitness test' too. A fitness test does just that, it attempts to gauge your current fitness level. Anyone who is embarking upon an exercise programme really needs to know with reasonable accuracy where they are starting from.

Fitness tests vary from the highly elaborate, as found in a clinical setting, to more simple, but still accurate (if carried out by a trained technician) assessments in most health clubs and gymnasiums, to useful and reasonably accurate assessments which you can determine at home. To be of any worth, a fitness assessment needs to take all the health related components of fitness into account.

A 'field' fitness test, such as is now found increasingly in health clubs usually looks at the various components of fitness as follows. Cardiorespiratory efficiency is usually estimated according to how well you perform on a calibrated exercise cycle, or ergometer. How well you do is often related to population norms, which let you know whether you are excellent, above average, etc.

Muscular endurance and muscular strength are assessed either by using some form of grip dynamometers, or by assessing how well you perform certain exercises involving your body weight, on some form of resistance equipment, such as that featured in the exercise chapters of this book.

Flexibility is commonly assessed by seeing how far you can reach towards or past your toes from a seated position.

Body composition is more often than not, estimated by taking measurements at various skinfold sites around the body, and substituting the values obtained in an equation which, again, will give you a value, which relates to other people of the same age and sex.

Admittedly, these are simple tests, but what they may lack in accuracy, is made up by the fact that as a result of following your exercise programme, you will certainly see improvements in all of the measurements taken — improvements which are very important in motivating you to continue with your exercise routine.

Simple tests can be done at home, too. One of the easiest undoubtedly is to take all your clothes off in front of a full length mirror and take a good hard critical look at yourself. If you dare, get a friend to take a photograph of you. Note which bits hang out, are bigger than you think is normal, which bits look flabby and out of condition. Standing normally, what is your posture like? Are your shoulders slumped, lower back arched, or is your head jutting forward? Make a note of all the areas of the body which you think could do with attention — getting a good friend to be honest and help you out here is often worth the embarrassment, since it is very easy to fool, or kid yourself that all is well.

Next, see how much flesh you can grab at various parts of your body, such as the side of the waist, the back of your upper arm, just below your shoulder blades, your inner thigh. Are there big handfuls in these areas, or just a pinch? Make a rough note of how much you can grab.

These two simple tests, the mirror test and the pinch/handful test should give you a good idea of not only how much fat you are carrying around, but also your general posture and shape. If you can take a picture, so much the better, since it will give you something to compare with after you have been exercising for a few weeks — you'll be amazed at the difference.

Assessing your flexibility can be carried out in virtually the same way as is carried out in the gym. Sit with your legs straight out in front of you, feet flexed. With your arms outstretched, try to reach forward. Can you reach your toes with your fingertips? Or are you nowhere near them? Try to get a friend to measure the distance in front or the distance past your toes with a ruler, using your toes as the zero point. Make a note of this measurement for later comparison.

If you are going to follow one of the resistance exercise programme outlines in this book, measuring strength and endurance of various muscles or muscle groups is not of major importance, since you will see that you are getting stronger or acquiring more endurance as you follow your programme. For instance, if you compare your week one programme, with say, week twelve, you will see that on those exercises which are the same the weights you are now handling with ease will be much more than those you started with.

Assessing your aerobic fitness can be done at home too. Perhaps one of the most widely known home tests is the twelve-minute run as devised by Dr Kenneth Cooper. Basically, all you have to do is to see how far you can go by walking/jogging/running in twelve minutes. If possible, make sure the distance you travel is accurately measured, preferably by carrying out your test on an athletics track. Make a note of your distance, then compare it to the tables opposite to see how you compare with your age group. Keep this measurement for future comparison with later repeats of the test. Also make a note of how you feel about your body and how you feel about yourself before you begin exercising. Keep all your measurements and observations safe in one place. A table for writing down your assessment is included at the end of this chapter.

So now you know where you are starting from, and you have a good idea of what you need and what you want to achieve. But is it realistic? There are certain things you cannot change through exercise, and there are certain things which although they can be changed, will take a considerable amount of hard work. In general the more you work at it, provided you are doing the right things the more changes you will notice.

Aerobic fitness changes very quickly. Following any of the traditional aerobic programmes outlined in this book should bring about increases in your aerobic fitness of approximately 15-25 per cent in three months. The aerobic circuit weight training programme will more likely result in changes in aerobic fitness of some 10 per cent in three months.

Strength and endurance changes will be very marked. It is not unusual to be able to complete your initial exercise programme with twice the weights, twice as many times after three months of regular and systematic exercising, although some of these changes will be due to skill learning.

Flexibility tends to show marked changes: if you were an inch or two short of your toes, you should be able to reach them three months later. Body composition changes slowly with exercise alone. However, if you have balanced out your programme in the manner which will be described below in the exercise section, a general exercise programme should, after three months, leave you with firmer, more shapely and defined limbs and a more erect posture, with fewer sagging parts. Check this by repeating your exercise tests and comparing the values you get with your pre-exercise values.

All exercise adapatations occur more rapidly in those people who have never exercised before. The fitter you are, and the fitter you become, the smaller the measurable changes. Eventually a stage may come when to get any greater or noticeable change will mean that you will have to spend more and more time exercising — something which may be detrimental to other aspects of your life.

Exercise can become an obsession leading, in itself, to health problems.

It is worth making a note of the fact that once you have reached a level of fitness, and are happy with the new you, your shape and condition can be maintained with less exercise than it took to get to where you are now in the first place, as long as you continue to exercise at the same intensity for the same length of time, one or two sessions a week should keep you in top condition. And, should you stop exercising completely, take heart in the fact that the longer you spent acquiring your fitness level, the more gradual will be your demise to pre-exercise levels.

But what of those aspects of your shape which cannot be changed easily through exercise? Basically these are related to your body type. A summary of the various body types and their main features is given in the diagrams on the following pages. Everyone has a mixture of body types, with certain characteristics being dominant, making them predominantly of one or perhaps two body types. For instance, it is possible to be a mesomorphic ectomorph if you have a certain element of muscularity about your linear frame.

Highly ectomorphic individuals will find it difficult to put on muscle mass, and no amount of exercise will change theirs or anyone else's skeletal frame. Similarly, highly endomorphic types will find losing body fat more difficult than most. Reproportioning in both cases is possible following the principles outlined in the exercise section, but it is difficult. Highly mesomorphic types will find a tendency to put on muscle bulk if they perform a lot of strength work, and for the mesomorph to slim down his/her

THE ECTOMORPH

Thin, linear, frail
undernourished look

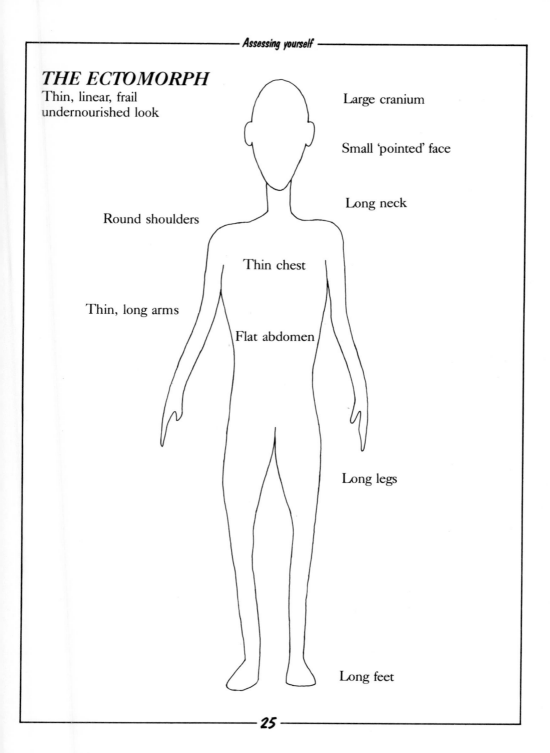

Large cranium

Small 'pointed' face

Long neck

Round shoulders

Thin chest

Thin, long arms

Flat abdomen

Long legs

Long feet

THE ENDOMORPH

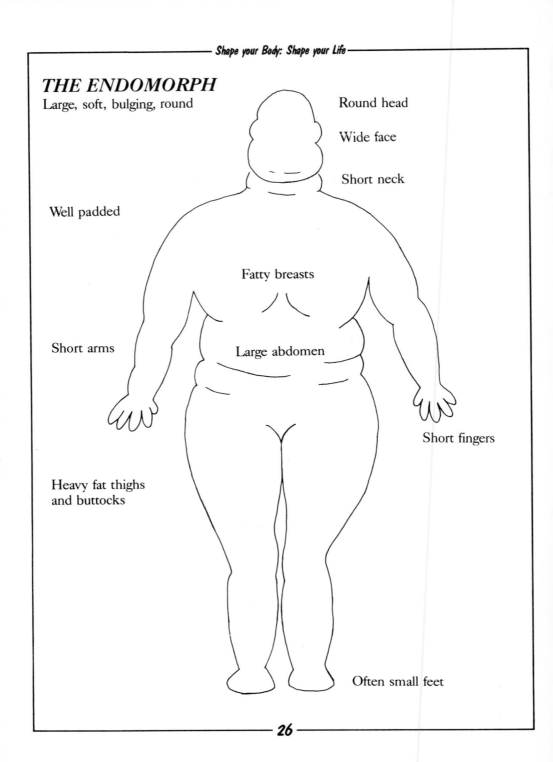

Large, soft, bulging, round

Round head

Wide face

Short neck

Well padded

Fatty breasts

Short arms

Large abdomen

Short fingers

Heavy fat thighs
and buttocks

Often small feet

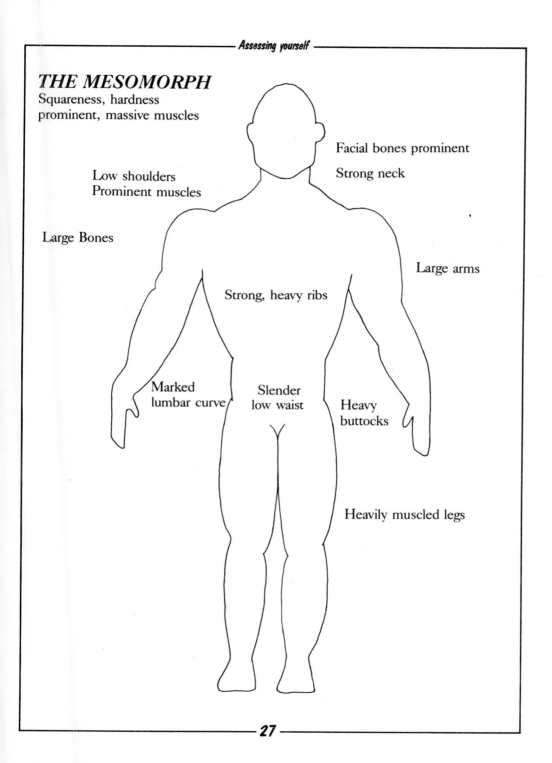

THE MESOMORPH
Squareness, hardness
prominent, massive muscles

Facial bones prominent

Strong neck

Low shoulders
Prominent muscles

Large Bones

Large arms

Strong, heavy ribs

Marked
lumbar curve

Slender
low waist

Heavy
buttocks

Heavily muscled legs

musculature is very unlikely.

Women have exactly the same possible combinations of body types as men, and they differ in their response to training only in that they have a much smaller tendency to increase their muscle bulk — their extra strength usually comes from an increase in the density of their muscles, and not their size. Muscle weight for muscle weight, women are as strong as men. The only women who are likely to increase greatly in their muscle size as a result of training are those who have high mesomorphic tendencies and have high male hormone levels.

Whatever your body type, and whatever your sex, no amount of exercise can change the width, depth or length of skeletal structures. In designing your programme, bear this in mind, you cannot make long legs out of short ones!

SELF ASSESSMENT RECORDING SHEET

Grab test

How much flab can you grab from the following sites?

Side of waist	Very little About an inch More than one inch A handful	Inner thigh	Very little About an inch More than one inch A handful
Upper arm	Very little About an inch More than one inch A handful	Below shoulder blades	Very little About an inch More than one inch A handful

Sit and reach test

(From a seated position on the floor, knees straight, how far forward can you reach?)

10 inches away from your toes
 5 inches away from your toes
 2 inches away from your toes
Just to your toes
 1 inch past your toes
 2 inches past your toes
 5 inches past your toes
10 inches past your toes

Mirror test

(Stand naked in front of a full length mirror then truthfully tick which descriptions apply to you, adding any general observations as necessary.)

	Before exercise	3 months	After 6 months	9 months
Head erect and balanced				
Head poking forward				
Shoulders level				
One shoulder higher than the other				
Both shoulders forward				
Chest up and slightly forward				
Chest depressed				
Flat abdomen				
Protruding abdomen				
Pelvis balanced				
Low back arched				
Spine curves sideways				
Substantial curving of the upper back				
Legs straight, knee caps facing forward				
Knock knees				
Bow legs				
Knees bent back				
Knees not fully straightened				
Parallel feet with domed arch				
Ankles rolling in				
Ankles rolling out				
Flabby appearance				
Firm appearance				

Mirror test
General comments

Twelve-minute run test

How far can you run/walk in twelve minutes? This simple testing procedure was originally devised by Dr Kenneth Cooper. (Charts reproduced with permission from *The New Aerobics* by Kenneth H. Cooper M.D., M.P.H., Bantam Books, 1970.)

Distance in miles covered in 12 minutes

Age (men)

Under 30	30-39	40-49	50+	Fitness Category
<1.0	<.95	<.85	<.80	Very poor
1.0–1.24	.95–1.14	.85–1.04	.80–.99	Poor
1.25–1.49	1.15–1.39	1.05–1.29	1.0–1.24	Fair
1.50–1.74	1.40–1.64	1.30–1.54	1.25–1.49	Good
1.75 +	1.65 +	1.55 +	1.50 +	Excellent

Age (women)

Under 30	30-39	40-49	50+	Fitness category
<.95	<.85	<.75	<.65	Very poor
.95–1.14	.85–1.04	.75– .94	.65– .84	Poor
1.15–1.34	1.05–1.24	.95–1.14	.85–1.04	Fair
1.35–1.64	1.25–1.54	1.15–1.44	1.05–1.34	Good
1.65 +	1.55 +	1.45 +	1.35 +	Excellent

General observations

How do you feel about yourself?

4

Designing your programme —
What type of exercise do you need?

Knowing that you are fit to exercise, and knowing what your realistic aims are from the previous section is all well and good — but what do you need to do to get the results you want?

Just as there are different components of fitness with different associated benefits, so you need to do different types of exercise to get those benefits. Further, the necessary exercise needs to be carried out at a certain intensity, for a certain length of time, and repeated with a certain regularity if you are to get maximum benefit and achieve your goals. Listed in terms of the components of fitness, the features of the exercise programme which you should follow in each case look like this:

1. EXERCISES FOR CARDIORESPIRATORY EFFICIENCY

Type of exercise
Any which causes you to have to breathe in and out more rapidly and raises your heart rate into a training zone (see appendix 2). The greater the number of muscles involved in the exercise, the better, since more muscles will demand to be supplied with more oxygen and nutrients, and will require substances which cause fatigue to be eliminated and dispersed — thus asking your cardio-respiratory system to do more work.

It is best if the muscles involved in the exercises are engaging in regular rhythmical movements (ie, they are contracting and relaxing alternately) since muscles which are held in a state of tension without causing movement (static or isometric contractions) can lead to elevated blood pressure throughout the duration of the exercise. The standard recommended activities for improving cardiorespiratory efficiency are: walking; jogging; running; cycling; aerobic dance; swimming — if you are a good swimmer; circuit weight training.

Intensity of exercise
Research is increasingly indicating that to be of benefit, exercise to improve cardiorespiratory efficiency does not have to be of high intensity. Beginners need only exercise at an intensity which leaves them comfortably out of breath, but still able to carry out a breathy conversation. Even if you are extremely fit in this respect working at or near your maximum will not bring you any extra benefit and may indeed not give you the results that you want.

Duration of exercise
This factor is linked with intensity of

exercise since the more intense the exercise, the shorter the length of time you will be able to keep doing it. Low to moderate intensity exercise of the type described will have benefits if you are extremely unfit with just a few minutes work. The average person should aim to progressively increase the duration of their chosen activity type to approximately thirty to sixty minutes (see sample programmes).

Frequency of exercise sessions

Any exercise is better than none, but to get steady improvement exercising around three times a week at equally spaced intervals is ideal for most people.

2. EXERCISE FOR MUSCULAR ENDURANCE

Type of exercise

Any which requires a muscle or group of muscles to repeatedly perform a task. Repeatedly performing an exercise obviously requires that the muscles in question are well backed up by the cardio-respiratory systems, and certainly all those muscles which are used in any of the exercise types listed under the previous component of fitness will improve their endurance. Those muscles which are not used, will not improve, so if you are engaging only lower body muscles in an activity, for example, the upper body muscles will need some similar type of work to 'balance out' the body, since imbalances in aspects of fitness can often in themselves lead to injury, and if not, often to some very odd shapes and postures.

Activities — all those as for cardio-respiratory efficiency. For individual muscles or muscle groups do some weight training or exercises using the weight of the body.

Intensity of exercise

Low: the very definition of muscular endurance signifies that the exercise needs to be repeated for a period of time. Working at low intensity means that you can continue to perform the activity for a long while. Guidelines to follow are those as for cardiorespiratory efficiency in activities involving large muscle groups. For single muscles worked using weights or body weight, the intensity should not be so great that you cannot perform at least 25 repetitions of the exercise in question, whilst still maintaining good technique.

Duration of exercise

Variable, since it depends upon the activity/exercise. In large muscle group activities, time is similar to cardio-respiratory efficiency of comparable types of exercise. For individual muscle group activities, the total time of exercise will depend upon the number of repetitions performed and the total number of exercises completed. A general endurance programme in a gymnasium setting can be completed comfortably in 45 minutes.

Frequency of exercise

For optimal results, three times a week at equally spaced intervals.

3. EXERCISE FOR MUSCULAR STRENGTH

Type of exercise

Any exercise which requires a muscle to overcome resistances which are maximal or near maximal. By saying this it is obvious that such work is placing a considerable amount of stress upon not only the muscles and associated structures such as tendons (which link muscles to bones) ligaments (which hold bones together) and other aspects of joints, but also the cardiovascular system. (Straining to lift heavy weights for instance can lead to a rise in blood pressure whilst the activity continues). Because of this, strength training work needs to be undertaken cautiously initially, and beginners are advised to follow a general conditioning programme for cardio-respiratory efficiency and muscular endurance prior to any intense strength work if they are to avoid injury. Activities: weight training.

Intensity of exercise

High to very high.

Duration of exercise

For each muscle or muscle group involved, the actual time spent training is very short indeed, because of the high intensity. In strength training for instance, an exercise may well be repeated only six times or less in one set. However, since several sets are necessary, often upwards of three, depending upon the system being used, for each muscle group, devoted strength trainees can often spend several hours in a gym!. The average member of the exercising public can achieve appropriate strength changes in the major muscle groups in approximately 45 minutes.

Frequency of exercise

For optimum results, repeat three to four times a week at equally spaced intervals.

4. EXERCISE FOR FLEXIBILITY

Type for exercise

Any exercise which takes muscles and joints into positions which they have never been in before, yet which are anatomically sound and possible. Forced and jerky movements should be avoided, since it is these which cause injury. The best type of movement to follow is one which progressively takes a limb or limbs into a position, and then requires you to hold that position. Before any type of stretching, the muscles and joints should be thoroughly warmed up (see warm up). Activities: yoga, stretch classes.

Intensity of exercise

Stretching exercises are difficult to describe in terms of intensity. You should feel that you are as far into the position that you are holding as you can go, without feeling that it is painful.

Duration of exercise

Each position needs to be held for approximately thirty seconds. Since a good flexibility programme needs to involve upper and lower body, front and back, the total time spent exercising can mount up. As part of a general exercise programme, a 'good stretch' can be achieved in fifteen minutes.

Frequency of exercise

As with other components of fitness,

optimal benefits can be achieved by repeating your stretch session three times a week, at equally spaced intervals.

5. *EXERCISE TO IMPROVE BODY COMPOSITION*

Type of exercise
Exercise which either concentrates upon using fat as fuel and thereby decreasing body fat, similar activities to those prescribed for cardiorespiratory efficiency, OR exercise which concentrates upon increasing muscle mass, as in certain heavy strength programmes. The former is probably more appropriate for the majority of people, and the more easily achieved.

Intensity of exercise (fat burning)
To use fat as fuel for exercise requires that you work at low intensity, but continuously, using large muscle groups in rhythmical contractions. Intensity of exercise is therefore low.

Duration of exercise
Significant amounts of body fat are only used as fuel for activity when you have been exercising continuously for at least thirty minutes. Hence your exercise should not be that intense that you cannot keep going for at least this time. Beginners are probably best advised to start with a long walk/jog.

Frequency of exercise
Four times a week at regularly spaced intervals will bring the most beneficial results. Remember though that if you have a great deal of body fat to lose, it is best combatted through a combination of diet and exercise.

SUMMARY: AIMS, NEEDS AND REALISTIC GOALS

By now various key aspects regarding the design of your exercise programme should be clear.

1. Every exercise programme should take you as the starting point.
2. Always assess your health status, by using a simple pre-exercise questionnaire (page 21) and/or get a medical check up if you are in any doubt as to your fitness to exercise.
3. Try to assess as accurately as possible your current fitness level — the simple home tests given on page 30 will do. Make a record of your performance on all the tests you carry out for later comparison to see the effectiveness of your exercise programme.

4. Understand clearly what it is possible to achieve with the exercise programme you are going to follow and make sure that your aims are realistic, according to your health, level of fitness, age, body type, sex, etc.

5. Your exercise programme must begin with less exercise, working up progressively to more exercise as the weeks go by (see sample programmes page 42). Do not overestimate your ability to do exercises, or your current fitness level!

5

Structuring your exercise session

You now know what you want and need to do, and you have a very good idea about how to go about it, in the sense that you know what form your exercise programme should take in general terms of type, intensity, duration and frequency of exercise. What you do not know yet is how to structure each individual exercise session so that it too has some form of logic and inherent safety.

Although it is probably true to say that many potential injury causing situations can be avoided by correct assessment of you and your needs, it is still very possible to harm yourself if you neglect to structure and carry out each individual exercise session according to fairly simple guidelines.

Dress

Always make sure that you are dressed appropriately for the activity you are about to do. Clothing should be loose and comfortable, allowing you considerable freedom of movement. As you exercise, you will find that you get warmer, hence it is better to dress in layers at the beginning of exercise which can be discarded as you get warmer. Correct footwear has been shown to be very effective in preventing all kinds of injury to the joints of the lower body. Make sure that you are wearing shoes which are designed for the activity in question, and that suit your feet. Take advice from your local sports shoe shop.

Warming up

Always warm up thoroughly. Warming up means just that — increasing the temperature of the body slightly and hence preparing it for subsequent activity. A small increase in the temperature of the body is beneficial for several reasons. Not only will muscles find it easier to contract and relax when they are warmer, but they, their tendons and other joint structures will be less likely to be damaged when you start exercising. Various processes involved in energy production also occur far more readily with a slight increase in temperature, and even nerve impulses travel far more rapidly.

All top athletes, and the majority of recreational exercisers also find that the time taken to warm up helps them to rehearse or prepare themselves for what they are going to do in their activity session.

Ideally you should try not only to increase the temperature of the body slightly, but also to take your limbs, joints and muscles through their current range of movement. Aim to involve large muscle groups as much as possible to begin with, since in the act of producing movement, muscles produce a lot of heat. In the gym or exercise studio this can be accomplished by jogging on the spot, stationary cycling, treadmill running, etc, all at slow speeds.

Use extra layers of clothing to help you get warm more quickly. You should then perform large rhythmical movements with your limbs, examples of which are given in the exercise section (Warming up), before moving on to light stretching activities, examples of which are also given. Make sure that any muscles or joints that are going to be doing specific or prolonged movements or activities should receive particular attention in your warming up phase. Runners, for example, might want to spend more time performing hamstring and calf stretching.

Most people should spend 10-15 minutes warming up but the older and/or more unfit should spend longer, approximately 20 minutes.

Technique

Always make sure that you are performing every exercise you do in the right way. Poor technique invariably leads to injury, so get it right from the beginning. Technical pointers and instructions are given with all the exercises featured in this book — make sure that you read them, as well as looking at the pictures!

When doing any kind of weight training it is tempting to try and lift heavier weights, or to move too quickly. You should never sacrifice technique to lift heavier weights or to lift weights more quickly — you will not get the results you want, and you will end up injured and unable to exercise if you do.

Balance your programme

Endeavour to make sure that you are not working components of fitness, certain muscles groups, parts of the body, etc, to the exclusion or detriment of other components of fitness, or other parts of the body. A programme which is unbalanced will lead to an unbalanced body.

Warming down

At the end of any exercise session you should always bring your body back down to normal as much as possible. However following any exercise in which many muscles have been doing lots of work, your body will be very warm indeed. Since muscles and joints respond best to any flexibility work when they are thoroughly warm, now is the best time to do the bulk of your flexibility work.

Avoid sitting or lying on the floor immediately after strenuous activity since this can impede your recovery from exercise. It is better and safer to continue moving rhythmically, albeit at a much lower intensity until your heart rate and rate of breathing are nearer normal before going down on the floor to do any stretches.

Because your body will start to cool fairly rapidly once you have stopped exercising, it is probably a good idea to replace some of the clothing you removed when you started to get too warm!

Listen to your body

Many exercisers tend to ignore one of the most important safety devices they have — their own body. Because of the numerous ways the body has of knowing exactly what is going on, it often knows when things are wrong and tells you so. Unfortunately, most of us tend to ignore our own body's advice.

Simple rules to follow

If you feel any pain at all, stop what you are doing and seek advice. Feeling uncomfortable is common if you have not exercised for a long time, but pain is a distinct warning that something is wrong. any of the following signify over-exertion: nausea; light-headedness; mental confusion; rapid or irregular breathing patterns; skin pallor; inability to maintain a normal movement pattern; un-steadiness.

Extreme soreness or tenderness one or two days after exercising also mean that you have done too much in your exercise session — reduce the intensity next time.

Other common sense rules include not exercising if you feel at all unwell or below par, or if you have just eaten a heavy meal or had several alcoholic drinks.

Progress

There are no hard and fast rules regarding how quickly each person should progress with their exercise programmes. Several guidelines can be given however.

1. Always move at your speed, listening to your body as you go along.
2. The older you are, the slower in general will be your progress.
3. All exercise requires a degree of skill learning. As you learn the skills associated with each exercise you will find your progress most rapid. Once you have perfected the skills involved in the exercises, progress will be less rapid. A beginner to weight training will find that he/she will be increasing the weights lifted in leaps and bounds for the first few weeks, then much more slowly from then on — this should be expected and does not

mean that you are not making further progress rather that you have learned how to do the exercise most efficiently. After this early learning phase (usually two to four weeks) more profound changes begin to take place within the body.

Terms used in training and exercise.

Repetition: one complete execution of an exercise, from start to finish.

Set: the number of repetitions of an exercise, carried out one after the other.

Circuit: a number of sets of different exercises.

The terms relating to the contraction of muscles are best explained by understanding how muscles produce movement. Very simply, the bones of the body act as a series of levers, which can move according to how they meet at the different joints. Muscles are attached to bones by connective tissues known as tendons which run continuously around and through the whole muscle.

For movement to take place, one end of the muscle must attach 'above' a joint, and one end of the muscle must attach 'below' the same joint. When a muscle is given an appropriate nerve impulse, various changes occur within the cells of the muscle which result in the muscle trying to bring its ends together. In other words, it starts to shorten. Because the ends of the muscle are attached to bones, the shortening of the muscle brings the bones together, and movement at the joint which the muscle spans is the result.

When a muscle shortens in this way, it is said to be contracting concentrically. Yet a muscle can also attempt to shorten, but come against resistance, such that the bones or limbs do not move. In this case this type of contraction is known as static, or isometric. Muscles can also control the

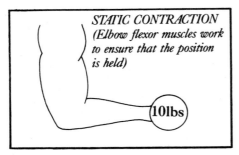

STATIC CONTRACTION
(Elbow flexor muscles work to ensure that the position is held)

10lbs

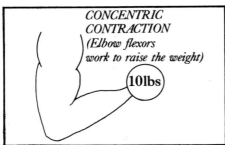

CONCENTRIC CONTRACTION
(Elbow flexors work to raise the weight)

10lbs

starting position. Remember though, that many other muscles besides just the ones involved in the exercise will also be working, often statically to maintain the position of the rest of your body so that you can carry out your chosen exercise. Some trainers also refer to concentric contractions as

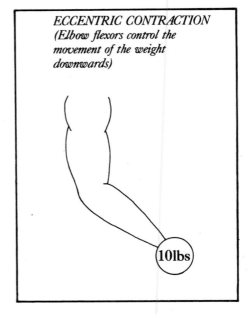

ECCENTRIC CONTRACTION
(Elbow flexors control the movement of the weight downwards)

10lbs

movement of bones or limbs from their shortened position back to their original resting length. When the muscle gradually lengthens, whilst at the same time controlling a movement, this is known as an eccentric contraction. Examples are given in the diagrams above.

In most exercises you will find that the muscles involved will contract concentrically in raising a weight or body part, then contract statically as the weight or body part is held or maintained in a certain position, then contract eccentrically as the weight or body part is gradually lowered back to the

being 'positive' work, with eccentric contractions being referred to as 'negative' work.

It is also possible for muscles to contract isokinetically. This means that they cause a joint to change its angle at a constant rate. Since muscles are able to overcome resistance with a varying ability depending upon characteristics of muscle, bone and joint arrangements, and how quickly the muscle is having to shorten, real isokinetic contractions can only be achieved using highly sophisticated equipment, the most famous being that produced by Cybex.

6
Types of equipment

There are currently many different types of equipment to use for resistance training. Initially, you can start at the very simplest level with just your own body weight — and many of the exercises featured in the exercise section will show you how to do this effectively.

Still at a simple level you can use dumb-bells and barbells, or strap on wrist and ankle weights to provide extra resistance, and a greater variety to the number of exercises you can do. Dumb-bells are basically just steel rods to which weight discs, usually made of iron, are added and secured in place with a collar. A barbell is a longer steel rod, more suitable for handling heavier weights and doing symmetrical work, to which the weights are attached and secured, again with collars.

These days, barbell and dumb-bells come in a variety of forms: some are chrome plated (the most expensive) some rubber or vinyl coated (for floor safety). Some come in sets and are fixed so that you cannot add or remove weights from their ends — these are the type most commonly found in health clubs. Most barbell and dumb-bell kits sold in shops come with a selection of discs of different weights so that you can make up your dumb-bells and barbells as required for your needs.

Many, many exercises can be done with the basics described, though some exercises will require adjustable benches or weight stands for their execution.

At a slightly more advanced level, much of the equipment you are likely to find in a health club will feature a weight stack: that is a block of weights whose movement occurs up and down steel guide-rails. The weight you require is selected by adjusting the position of a steel selector pin in the weight stack. The weights are moved via a cable and pulley system, usually, although lever arrangements are also very common. Arguably, such weight stack systems are very safe, since you never directly pick up weights, but it is still possible to injure yourself if you ignore correct exercise technique. Such exercise equipment can be arranged in the form of single exercise 'stations' or grouped together as a multigym, allowing several people to exercise at the same time.

More sophisticated versions of traditional weight stack equipment exist. The equipment described so far relies upon constant resistance. In other words, the weight you are using does not change throughout the exercise. But as indicated in the section describing how muscle produces movement, a muscle is capable of developing more or less force, and therefore working at different intensities, according to mechanical factors, basic characteristics and how quickly it shortens. In the light of this, various manufacturers have incorporated cams, levers or clutches into their equipment design so that the resistance you are having to overcome changes according to the amount of force you can develop at different joint angles and speeds. Theoretically, such equipment should allow you to work equally hard throughout your full range of movement. In practice, individual differences make the design of an exercise machine along these lines impractical for large consumer use. However, current ranges are very good indeed, especially if you follow manufacturers' instructions regarding how you should position yourself, and the speed at which you should carry out each exercise.

More recent equipment designs incorporate hydraulic cylinders to provide the resistance as opposed to the more traditional weight stack. In carrying out the exercise, the fluid contained in the cylinder is forced through an aperture — the smaller the aperture (governed by a dial) and the more quickly you try to perform the exercise, the greater the force you must overcome. Most hydraulic based apparatus allows you to do concentric work only, the return movement of an exercise being carried out by concentric contraction of the opposing muscle group. This has led some manufacturers to claim that their equipment is double-positive in its action, and that your exercise routine can be carried out in half the time that more conventional weight stack equipment would require. Such claims have not been fully substantiated by independent research work. The absence of eccentric work also gives rise to claims that muscle soreness following exercise is unheard of with concentric only exercising. Whilst eccentric exercise is strongly implicated in delayed muscle soreness high intensity concentric work can also produce similar problems. If you have designed your programme well, according to the guidelines given, delayed muscle soreness or acute stiffness will never be a problem, whichever method of training you are following.

For general conditioning and variety, it is probably best to incorporate body weight, free weight and different types of exercise equipment into your programme designs. More recent equipment may be more visually attractive and appealing, and perhaps make it possible to do certain exercises more efficiently and safely but it is the work you do that matters, since no machine will do the work for you!

7

Safety rules when using free weights, or weight training equipment

One of the most important safety rules when using any kind of weight training equipment is to always exercise with correct technique. You should always exercise from a firm base, particularly in free standing exercises. When lifting weights off the floor, lift as you would any heavy object: by bending your knees and keeping your back straight and long. This applies equally to putting weights down again, too.

Remember to breathe regularly (as indicated in the technical description accompanying each exercise depicted in the exercise section).

Always check any equipment you are about to use. With free weights, barbells and dumb-bells, make sure that all collars are on and tightened, and that the bar is balanced by having equal amounts of weight on each end. If you are using a bench or stands, make sure that they are stable, and/or adjusted to the right height. If you are adding or removing weights from a bar, make sure it is on the floor.

When doing awkward, overhead, or prone exercises with weights, always get the help of a friend. In general it is safer (and often more fun) to exercise with a partner.

Make sure that you are always in control of the weight you are using, that you execute all movements smoothly and without jerking, and when using free weights, that bars move in a parallel and stable manner — they should not wobble.

With equipment which has a weight stack, always ensure that the pin in the weight stack is in the right place for you, and that it is secure. Always adjust seat heights and/or lever arm lengths to suit your body — instructions vary according to the range of equipment you are using — check with the gym, health club or manufacturers' instructions.

Never put your hands or feet in or under weight stacks, and ensure that your body parts stay well away from any moving parts of machinery which are unguarded or exposed.

8

Choosing your exercises

The exercise section of this book is split into different parts according to how your session should be structured. All exercisers should begin with a warm up. The first section gives the guidelines for constructing your warm up, and a sample warm up session. The resistance exercises themselves are then listed in terms of the parts of the body which are involved. Some exercises involve no equipment, some involve simple equipment, and some involve equipment such as would be found in a health club or gymnasium.

According to your circumstance and how you want to emphasize your programme, choose exercises for each major body part, from these sections. Sample programmes are given under appropriate headings. The sections for each body part include more than one exercise precisely because having a choice of exercises for the same body part enables you to build variety and interest into your exercise programme as the months go by. All the possible combinations of exercises and methods of exercising should leave you with enough exercise programmes to last for many years!

The exercise section ends with exercises for warming down, including stretching, again with guidelines.

SAMPLE PROGRAMME PROFILES

This section deals with sample programmes, and includes programmes which has been designed for representative people. Simple and highly accessible aerobic programmes which do not involve specialized equipment (walking and jogging) are included precisely because such activities provide an excellent means of burning up calories and complement any weight training programme, as well as providing a means of slowly and gradually introducing your body to regular exercise. If you are a regular swimmer or cyclist, for walking or jogging read swimming or cycling.

Reading through all of the sample programmes and profiles should give you a good idea of the immense variety which weight training offers, as well as showing you how (if by now you need any more help!) to put your own individual weight training programme together.

Sample programmes: aerobic fitness
Walking
Suitable for absolute beginners — those people who have not taken part in any

regular physical activity for a number of years. Improves cardiorespiratory efficiency and local muscular endurance of the legs — does little for the upper body, or for flexibility. Carried out for long enough on a regular basis, this recreation can help with weight control (see body composition).

Technical points: use the whole of the foot when walking, pushing off firmly from the back leg. Make sure you wear good shoes. Walk 'tall'.

Programme guidelines: Start off with 15 minutes of continuous walking 3 times a week. Add around 3-5 minutes to each walk each week, until you are walking briskly for an hour, 3 times a week. Vary your routes as much as possible.

Jogging

Simple, accessible and highly aerobic, just like walking. Good for cardiorespiratory efficiency and muscular endurance of the legs, and for 'fat burning' if carried out for long enough, often enough. Does little for upper body, or for flexibility.

Technical points: Invest in a good pair of shoes by going to a specialist shoe shop and asking for advice. Wear loose fitting and comfortable clothing, and keep extremities covered in cold or windy conditions. Use the whole of your foot on each stride, run tall with upper body relaxed.

Programme guidelines: Absolute beginners should start off with a walking programme, continuing this for approximately 4 weeks. Then break up your walking time with periods of slow jogging for as long as you feel comfortable, returning to walking as necessary. Repeat each session 3 times a week, gradually extending the time spent jogging and

decreasing the time spent walking. Aim to increase your jogging time by two minutes each week until you are jogging continuously for around 40 minutes on each outing, 3 times a week.

Walking and jogging programmes

Warming up

Whilst it is perhaps not so crucial to warm up for walking briskly, or for jogging slowly as it is for running, some light mobilization work such as that recommended in the warm up section for weight training is advisable, especially light stretching of the calves (page 60).

Following the walk or jog, again go through some of the stretches in the stretching section, particularly those involving the legs, hips and buttocks.

If you have progressed to the extent that you are now running (Men — faster than 8 minutes per mile, Women — faster than 9 minutes per mile) it would be advisable to carry out all the mobilizing and preparatory work in the warm up section, before your run, and all the stretching work in the warming down section following your run.

Sample programmes using weights

Circuit weight training

An excellent all round method of enhancing all components of fitness if carried out correctly. The whole body can be worked and there are numerous ways of varying the sessions to get different benefits as required, and to suit different individuals.

What is it? Generally anything between 10 and 16 exercises are arranged in a sequence, usually alternating upper and lower body exercises. It is common to work for 30 seconds on a general programme on each exercise. The exercise should be carried out using weights (free weights or machines) which are around half that of the maximum weight you could possibly lift for that exercise. Each exercise should be carried out smoothly for the allotted time, such that some 15-20 repetitions are performed on each exercise.

Having completed one set of repetitions on the first exercise, you should move quickly either to the next exercise in the circuit, or for greater aerobic benefit, to approximately 30 seconds of stationary cycling, treadmill running or some other form of traditional aerobic exercise, then move onto the next exercise. With increasing fitness, the circuit can be completed more times, usually a maximum of 3 complete circuits.

Variety can be introduced by changing the exercises, the length of the exercising time, the length of the recovery or aerobic exercise time, the weights, etc.

If heavier weights are used, the circuit influences strength more, if lighter weights are used, the circuit will emphasize muscular endurance and cardiorespiratory fitness more.

Technical points: correct technique must be followed at all times.

If a warm up and warm down is included with each session, including flexibility work, then such a session constitutes an excellent all round fitness session which can be completed easily within 45-60 minutes.

Sample programmes for local muscular endurance.

General — similar in benefit to circuit weight training with light weights.

Aim to use weights sufficiently light that 25 or more repetitions can be completed on each exercise.

Sample programmes: muscular strength

Weights should be sufficiently heavy on each exercise that certainly no more than 10 repetitions can be completed for each exercise. After one set of exercises has been completed, take a short rest of approximately 60 seconds, then repeat the exercise set. After another short break repeat the set. Between three and four sets are the usual with anything between 6 and 10 repetitions of each exercise for general strength gains.

Exercise all muscle groups in a similar way, structuring your session such that larger muscle groups are exercised first.

There are literally hundreds of different systems in operation which can bring about changes in strength — bodybuilders and power and strength athletes will follow very rigorous and intense systems indeed. If this is your specific aim, consult a bodybuilding manual. For most people aiming for marked strength improvements, 4 sets of 6 repetitions of the heaviest weight you can perform the exercise with, has been found to be very effective as a training system.

Your starting weight

How do you know which weight is right for you on each exercise? The straight answer is that it is a case of trial and error. Obviously, smaller muscles can handle smaller weights than larger muscles can, but picking the right weight for each exercise not only depends upon you, your level of fitness, sex, etc, but also what you are exercising for. In the programme guidelines you will see that no weights are given, rather a number of repetitions and sets are given. The weight you choose for each exercise should be such that you can carry out that number of sets and repetitions as stated with your chosen weight. If you cannot, the weight is too heavy, if you can with ease, it is probably too light.

Similarly, when a number of sets and repetitions becomes very easy, it is time to increse the weight for that exercise, unless you are happy with your level of fitness, in which case you should keep that weight the same.

It is better on your first few sessions as a beginner to err on the side of caution, and start with a weight which is lighter than you think you can handle.

SAMPLE PROGRAMMES — NORMAL PEOPLE AND THEIR REQUESTS

Profile:

JD. A 25-year-old female journalist. Her work means that she is desk bound for the majority of the day and she gets little exercise as a result of her occupation. Whilst not being over fat as such, she feels that she has become flabby especially around the buttocks and thighs. Being tied to her desk also means that she has recently begun to slouch over her typewriter, leading to poor posture. Working for a health magazine her knowledge of nutrition is sound and her diet is fine.

Recommendation:

Since JD had not exercised for such a long time she was recommended to begin a walking programme for a few weeks, which could easily fit into her lunch time. She had been thinking for some time about joining her local health club and this she did. Her initial programme was a general muscular endurance programme as follows:

General warm up: 15 minutes
Leg press machine
Chest press machine

Pulldown
Thigh extension
Thigh curl
Seated press
Bicep curl
Hip abduction machine
Hip adduction machine
Basic curl up
Diagonal curl up

Warm down and stretching: 15 minutes.

Her instructions were to complete 25 repetitions of each exercise maintaining good form and technique.

On her first session, she did each exercise 25 times, moving swiftly from one exercise to the next. As each session went by she extended the exercise session by repeating exercises, so that at the end of 3 weeks exercising 3 times a week she found herself doing her exercise circuit three times in total. She only increased the weights on any exercise when 25 repetitions was very comfortable.

After six weeks, JD adapted her programme so that it became more of a circuit training schedule. Her walking programme she then modified so that it became a jogging programme, and optimistically she entered a fun run three months into the future and began training for that. For variety, one of her circuit weight training sessions is substituted for one of her earlier muscular endurance programmes. Regularly, JD creates change by substituting different exercises for the same body part.

Profile:

AS. A 19-year-old male clerical worker. His work is predominantly sedentary, although cycling the 4 miles to work and back each day gives him some exercise. AS is underweight by a few pounds and feels weak. Posture is fine. He would like to put on some more muscle mass and just generally feel stronger.

Recommendation:

Not having done any weight training before, AS began his training programme by joining a local health club in easy cycling distance from his home. Here after a fitness test he began a general muscular endurance programme to familiarize himself and his body to weight training. After 4 weeks on this general programme, (exercising 3 times a week), AS changed to a strength programme. This he did by keeping the exercises the same as for his endurance programme, but increasing the weights which he had been using so that he could only just manage to do 4 sets of 6 repetitions on each exercise with good technique, allowing himself approximately 60 seconds between sets and exercises. Each time he trains, AS always makes sure he is working with slightly increased weights so that he is always exercising at high intensity. For variety, and aerobic fitness, once a week he does a circuit

weight training session.

AS has also modified his diet according to the guidelines given in the nutrition section.

AS General programme
Warm up 15 minutes
Leg press machine
Heel raise
Chest press machine
Pullover
Thigh extension
Thigh curl
Seated press
Bicep curl
Tricep press
Side lateral raises
Basic curl up
Diagonal curl up

Warm down and stretching 15 minutes

(Each exercise carried out with a light weight such that 20 repetitions of each exercise can be completed. Weight on each exercise is only increased when 20 repetitions is very easy and 3 circuits can be carried out with ease.)

AS Strength programme
Warm up 15 minutes
Half Squat
Heel Raise
Thigh extension
Thigh curl
Bench press
Dumb-bell flyes
Pulldown (wide grip)
Seated press
Upright rowing
Side lateral raises
Biceps curl
Tricep press
Curl up (Incline)

Diagonal curl (Incline)
Crunch

4 sets of 6 reps on all exercises (except abdominals, 4 sets of 15).

Profile:
CW. A 30-year-old sales manager (male). His work involves a lot of travelling and when he gets home he has no desire to go out again to a health club or exercise facility. He was formerly very active, but for the last 5 years has done very little in the way of systematic physical activity. Feels in need of a general exercise programme.

Recommendations:
Since CW has the space and the motivation to exercise at home, this was the obvious choice. He thus went out and bought a medium weight barbell and dumb-bell kit which he keeps in a spare room. He carries out a general muscular endurance programme when at home, which he supplements with a jogging programme in the park opposite his house. When away on business, he carries out as much of his warm up, warm down and free standing exercises without equipment, as possible.

General programme
Warm up 15 minutes
Half squat
Heel Raise
Press up
Upright rowing
Seated press
Alternate dumb-bell curl
Dips (between the backs of chairs)
Side lateral raises
Basic curl up

Diagonal curl up

Warm down 15 minutes

Profile:
ROC. A 40-year-old female executive. Again, the predominantly sedentary nature of her job means that ROC gets little physical activity in the course of her occupation. She has noticed that she has started to put on a little weight in the last two years even though she feels her eating habits have not changed, but it is true that she no longer swims on such a regular basis as she used to. Neither she nor her husband would like to join a health club.

Recommendation:
Although her eating habits may not have changed, ROC's level of activity has — from swimming on a very regular basis (3 times weekly) to hardly once a week now. By ensuring that she does swim at least once a week, and by beginning a social walking programme with her husband, ROC can tackle the aerobic aspect of her exercise schedule.

Since both she and her husband are keen to improve their fitness on all levels they invested in a home gym which they installed along with an exercise bicycle in the spare room in their bungalow. Using this equipment they follow a circuit weight training programme, concentrating upon 30 seconds work on each of the exercise stations of their multigym, followed by 30 seconds on their bicycle. Generally, they include 12 exercises in their circuit, and over the weeks have worked up to completing 3 circuits in all. They also use the home gym for specific strengthening work, ROC concentrating on upper back activities such as the pulldown for her posture.

Being 'aware' as you exercise

Some people are so intent on carrying out their exercise programme that they sometimes forget what they are supposed to be doing, or, equally frequently, are not fully aware of what they are doing. Make sure that besides looking at the illustrations that you read the accompanying caption and take heed of any pointers regarding positioning of limbs and body parts. Correct technique is not only essential to avoid injury but also necessary to get the most out of your exercise programme. Try visualizing where your body is and what it is doing as you carry out each exercise, becoming conscious of yourself and what your body is saying. Increasing your body awareness is one of the most important steps in making sure that you maximize your training time.

Breathing

There are a number of guidelines regarding breathing which you should follow when exercising. Firstly, always breathe regularly. Beginners have a tendency to stop breathing when they are learning new exercises — watch out for this.

Generally speaking, you should breathe out on the effort phase of an exercise, and in on the return movement. If an exercise involves your chest expanding, breathe in.

Instructions are given with each exercise.

Exercise — speed of movement

For general conditioning, exercise at a speed which allows you to be in control of your body at all times. Do not rush exercises. Muscles are conditioned most appropriately if you allow one or two seconds for both the concentric and eccentric phases of the exercise.

9

The warm up

Your warm up should last 10-15 minutes. Older and more unfit individuals should spend 15-20 minutes on this phase.

Posture

It is always a good idea to check your posture prior to exercise since exercising with poor posture only exacerbates your faults, and may lead to injury. Your feet should be a comfortable distance apart, about hip width, with your weight evenly balanced. Your shoulders should be down away from your ears and you should be looking forward. Your spine should feel lengthened from your tail right up to your head.

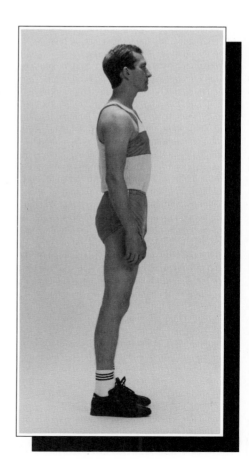

Shoulder circles

Having adjusted your posture, take your feet slightly wider apart to give you a more stable base. Keeping your arms down, lift your shoulders up towards your ears, then press them backwards as you bring them back to their resting position. Breathe comfortably throughout. Repeat 12 times.

Arm circles (single)

Standing in the same position as in the previous exercise, take one arm backwards in a giant circle. Your body should not move since the action takes place only at the shoulder joint. Your upper arm should brush your ear. Breathe comfortably throughout. Repeat 12 times on each side.

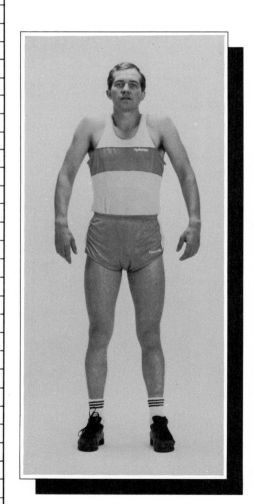

Arm circles (double)

Repeat as for the previous exercise, but take both arms back at the same time. All circling movements should be carried out under control and should not be forced or jerked.

Head turns

From your standing position in the previous exercise, turn your head so that you look first to one side, and then to the other, feeling the stretch in the neck. Your spine should be long throughout the exercise. Breathe comfortably, repeating the exercise 6 times on each side.

The exercise can be varied so that the head comes forward onto the chest before going to the other side, effectively completing an arc.

If you ever tilt your head backwards, make sure that you are controlling the movement, and that you are not allowing the head to fall back. Backward movements of the head should be carried out with care.

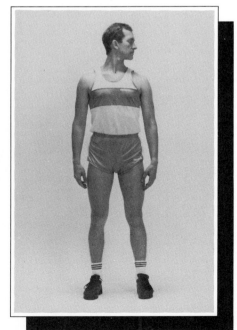

Arm running

From a good standing position, bring one arm forward and take the other arm back at the same time as if you are running. Make this an easy, comfortable swing of the arms, breathing comfortably throughout the exercise.

Repeat 12 times on each arm. Allow your knees to bend with the movement if you find this more appropriate.

Shoulder blade squeeze

From a good standing position and maintaining a long spine with shoulders down, place your interlocked hands on the small of your back. Now try to bring your elbows together behind you so that they almost touch, without arching your spine. Hold this position for a couple of seconds, then release and repeat 12 times, breathing easily throughout. You will feel a stretch in the muscles at the front of the chest if you are doing this correctly.

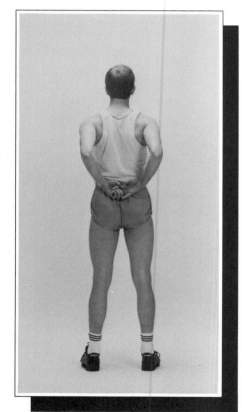

Reach for the ceiling

Stand tall with good posture and reach up to the ceiling with one arm so that you feel the stretch down one side of the body. You will find this more comfortable if you bend the knee on the side of the outstretched arm. (Do ensure that your knee follows the same line as the toes when you do this.) Hold the stretch momentarily, before repeating on the other side. Breathe comfortably throughout the sequence, reaching up 12 times on each side.

Side bends

Stand tall with feet a comfortable distance apart and with your hands on your hips, your spine long, lift up and away from your hips and bend to one side as if you are bending over a barrel placed under your armpit. Do not lean forwards or backwards. Breathe out as you bend to the side, and in as you return.

Repeat 12 times on each side.

Waist Twists

Stand as for the previous exercise, but with your knees slightly bent. Now smoothly twist your upper body round as far as possible without jerking, yet making sure that your hips are always facing forward. You should still have feeling of length in your spine.

Breathe easily throughout the exercise, repeating the sequence 12 times on each side.

Hip circles

Stand tall with your feet slightly wider than shoulder distance apart, hands on hips. From this position, smoothly swing your hips to the side, then to the back, to the other side and finally back to the front, having prescribed a large circle with your hips. Avoid jerkiness, breathing easily throughout and repeat 12 times in both directions.

Knees to chest

Stand tall. Maintain your upright and balanced stance as you bring one knee upwards to meet the elbow of the opposite arm — bend the knee of the supporting leg if you find it more comfortable. Repeat on the other side, then repeat the whole sequence 12 times, breathing easily throughout.

Leg swings

Stand tall with good posture, sideways on to a chair or bar. Rest one hand on the support for balance. Rest your other hand on your hip or hold it out to the side, whichever is more comfortable. Now swing your outside leg forward and backward without jerking. This should be a nice flowing, rhythmical movement. Avoid the temptation to over-arch the spine. Breath easily throughout and repeat the exercise 12 times on each side.

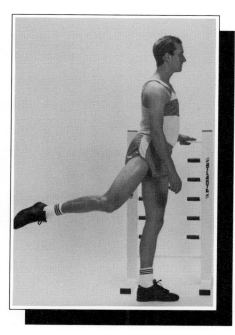

Half squats

Stand tall, feet about shoulder width apart, with hands either resting on your hips, or placed out in front of you for balance. From this position, bend at the knees and hips so that your thighs approach a parallel position with the floor, whilst still keeping your back long. Breathe in as you descend, and out as you rise.

Make sure that your knees follow the same line as your toes, and that you fully straighten your legs when you return to the standing position. Repeat 24 times.

If you feel unstable because your heels leave the floor as you squat, stand with your heels on a block of wood, approximately 1 inch high, or on two weight discs.

Skiing

Stand tall with good posture. Reach up with both arms until they are high above your head, then swing them down and squat at the same time, still keeping the back long, and your knees following the same line as your toes. When your thighs are about parallel with the floor, swing your arms forward and begin to straighten up until you are back in an upright position with your arms stretched up above your head.

The whole sequence should be fluid and rhythmical and should be repeated 24 times.

Breathe as for the half squat.

Forward lunge

Stand with one leg forward and one leg back, but keeping a long spine. Feet should be parallel and hip width apart, hands either resting on hips or by your sides.

Bend the knee of the leading leg so that it moves to a position approximately over the toe, still keeping the knee in line with the foot. Your back leg should remain straight, with your heel pressed into the floor.

Return to the starting position and repeat the movement 12 times on each side, breathing easily throughout.

Side lunge

Start with your legs wide apart, with one leg turned out from the hip so that the foot points along a diagonal, and with the other leg turned so that the foot faces directly forward.

Bend the knee of the turned out leg so that it ends up over the foot and pointing in the same direction — you will feel the stretch along the inner thigh of the other leg but keep the leg straight. Hold momentarily, before returning to your starting position

Repeat 12 times on each side, breathing easily throughout.

Hamstring stretch
(knees on chest)

Stand tall with your legs together. Now bend your knees and curl your spine down until your chest is resting on your thighs. In this position wrap your arms around the backs of your legs. Then attempt to straighten your legs whilst still keeping your chest on your thighs. Hold the nearly straightened position momentarily before bending your knees to release.

Breathe easily throughout the exercise and repeat the whole sequence 6 times.

Calf stretch (gastrocnemius)

Stand at an incline to a wall or barre resting your weight on your hands opposite your shoulders as in the illustration. Place one leg forward, with the knee over the toe, with the other leg stretched out behind you, heel pressed into the floor. Your hips should face the wall at all times and your feet should remain hip distance apart. Gradually inch back your rear foot, still keeping the heel on the floor until you feel a stretch in the back calf. Hold this position for a few seconds, then release. Repeat 6 times for each leg, breathing easily throughout.

Calf stretch (soleus)

Position as for the previous exercise, but bend the knee of the back leg slightly, still keeping the heel pressed into the floor. You will feel the stretch lower down in the calf. Repeat and breathe as for the previous exercise.

Jogging in place

For generally increasing the temperature of the body, large muscle activities such as jogging are ideal. Jogging in place can be carried out as part of your warm up, although it can get boring and if it is possible to jog and cover distance, do so. Remember to have good and appropriate shoes on, always put your heels down with each step and run tall: do not run as if you are sitting down! Keep your upper body relaxed, hands loose. Remember that rebounders can take a lot of shock out of jogging and are useful if you are very heavy on your feet or if you are nursing certain injuries, the floor is not very resilient.

Stationary Cycling

Many regular exercisers find that exercise cycles are more fun that jogging on the spot to warm up with. Check that you have adjusted the seat height correctly so that your legs are almost fully extended on each downstroke, and that the handlebars are adjusted accordingly. A comfortable cycling speed is one of 50-70 revolutions of the crank per minute.

Many exercise cycles found in gyms offer a host of extras, from fitness tests through to mimicing hills. Take advantage of any extras and flashing lights to introduce variety to your warm up.

Other large muscle warming up activities include skipping and rowing. Whatever activity you choose: jogging, rebounding,

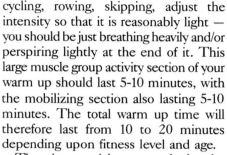

cycling, rowing, skipping, adjust the intensity so that it is reasonably light — you should be just breathing heavily and/or perspiring lightly at the end of it. This large muscle group activity section of your warm up should last 5-10 minutes, with the mobilizing section also lasting 5-10 minutes. The total warm up time will therefore last from 10 to 20 minutes depending upon fitness level and age.

There is some debate as to whether the mobilizing section or the large muscle group activity should come first. The warm up presented here is capable of being done either way. If you feel like it, or if the gymnasium situation dictates, either jog or cycle first, then mobilize, or the other way round.

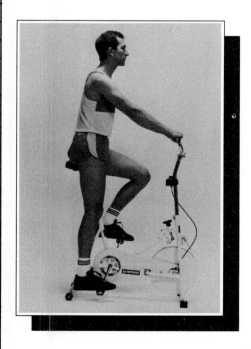

10

Exercises for the lower body

The exercises illustrated using equipment feature a representative selection of equipment which you are likely to find in any modern health club or gymnasium.* Just as there are many (some would say unlimited) exercises which can be performed with free weights, so there are many different pieces of modern single station exercise units. Whatever the manufacturer or type of equipment, always make sure you position yourself correctly on each piece of apparatus.

*The range featured in this section is that of Atlanta Sports Industries — the full range offered by Atlanta comprises some 27 machines in all, of which 14 are illustrated here.

Half squats
For the muscles of the legs and those around the hips and buttocks.

Stand tall with your feet hip width to shoulder width apart with a barbell sitting comfortably across the shoulders/upper back. Hold the bar firmly with a wide grip. Keeping your back flat throughout and your head in the same line as your spine, bend your knees, controlling your movement down. (It is neither necessary nor advisable to go down to a position lower than that illustrated to begin with. In general the lowest position you should attempt is one where your thighs are parallel to the ground). Return smoothly to your starting position making sure you fully straighten the legs.

If you feel unstable because your heels leave the floor as you squat, stand with your heels on a block of wood — approximately 1 inch high.

Breathe in as you descend, out as you rise.

Always make sure your knees follow the same line as your toes.

The machine version of this exercise is on either a leg press or duo squat machine.

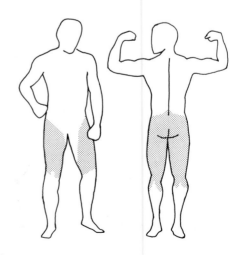

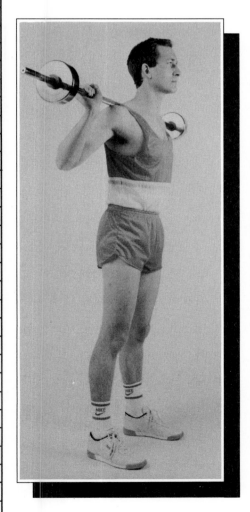

Heel raise
For the muscles of the calf.

Assume the starting position as for the half squat with a barbell resting across the shoulders/upper back. Then stand with the balls of your feet resting on a block of wood (or telephone directory), heels on the floor. Your legs should be straight. From this position, rise up on to your toes, hold momentarily, and then return to the starting position before repeating the sequence.

Breathe easily throughout.

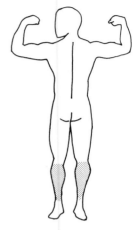

Kneeling kick back

For the muscles of the buttocks and backs of thighs.

Kneel on all fours, knees underneath hips, hands underneath shoulders. Bring one knee forward under your body rounding your back and bending your head at the same time so that knee and head almost touch. From this position push this leg out backwards behind you with a smooth action without arching your back. Keep your hips facing the floor throughout the exercise.

Breathe out as you bring the leg in, breathe in as you push the leg behind you.

Repeat on both legs.

Side leg lifts
For muscles on the outside of hip and thigh.

Lie on your side so that you have a straight line from ankle, knee, hip and shoulder. Rest your head on your lower arm and use your top arm as a support in front of your body. Keep your hips facing forward and smoothly raise your top leg, ensuring that the knee and foot of this leg always face forward. Avoid the tendency to roll forwards or backwards. Hold your uppermost position momentarily, then slowly lower to the starting position. As your ankles touch, repeat the sequence. Repeat on other side.

Breathe easily throughout.

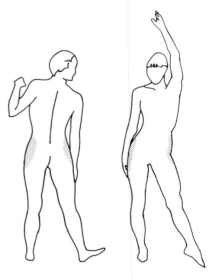

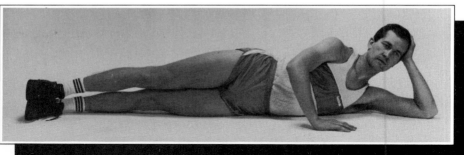

Lower leg lifts
For the muscles of the inner thighs.

Assume the side lying position as described in the previous exercise. This time however, bring the top leg over and forward of the lower leg.

Making sure that the hips are facing forward, lift the lower leg off the floor as high as possible, keeping the knee and foot of this leg also facing forward. Hold the top position momentarily then slowly lower. Just as the ankle touches the floor, repeat the sequence. Repeat on both sides, breathing easily throughout.

Heel raises (using the multi-exercise machine)
For the muscles of the calf.

Place the selector pin in the right position in the weight stack for you. Place the padded belt comfortably around your hips and hook the clip onto the lever arm of the machine, with knees bent and spine long. Stand on the appropriate step for your height with your heels off the edge. Now straighten your legs, still keeping your spine long so that the lever arm rises. From this position, with legs straight, rise up onto your toes, hold the topmost position for a moment, then control the movement so that your heels go down as far as possible beneath the level of the step. Repeat.

Breathe easily throughout.

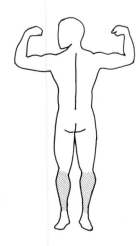

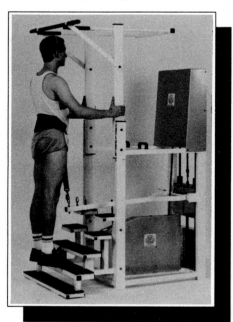

Thigh curl machine

For the muscles at the back of the thighs and calves.

Place the selector pin in the right position in the weight stack for you. Lie face down on the machine with your heels under the roller pads so that your knees are just off the edge of the bench and opposite the axis of rotation of the movement arm. Loosely grip the side handles. Keeping your hips pressed into the bench, bend your knees so that your heels come as close as possible to touching your buttocks. Hold your top position for a moment, then control the movement back to the starting position. Just as the weights touch the rest of the block, repeat. Keep your feet flexed throughout the exercise and breathe easily.

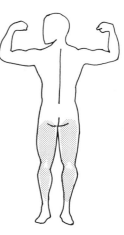

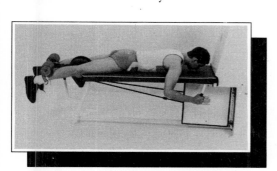

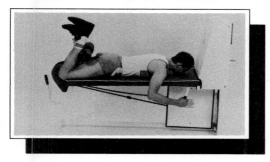

Thigh extension machine
For the muscles at the front of the thigh.

Place the selector pin in the right position in the weight stack for you. Adjust the position of the back rest so that when seated your knees are just off the edge of the bench with your lower back and shoulder pressed firmly into the support. Your ankles should be behind the roller pads. Loosely grasp the side handles. Maintaining this position, smoothly straighten both legs until they are fully extended. Hold this position momentarily, then slowly lower back to the starting position. Just as the weights touch, repeat.

Keep your lower back pressed into the support throughout the exercise, and keep the rest of your body relaxed.

This machine can be used to exercise one leg at a time.

Breathe easily throughout the exercise.

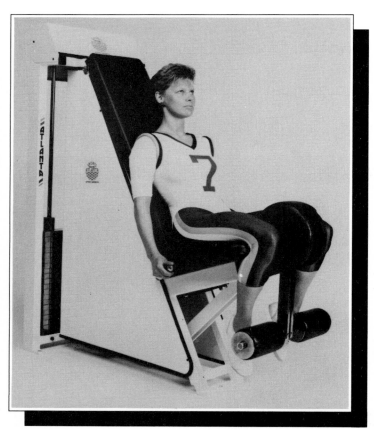

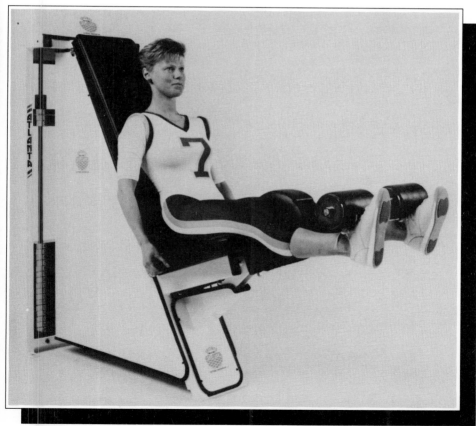

Hip adduction machine
For the muscles of the inner thigh.

Place the selector pin in the right position in the weight stack for you. Adjust the lever on the side of the machine to suit your range — the further round the lever is turned, the greater the range of movement.

Sit into the machine, pressing your back firmly into the support. Place your legs into the movement arms so that you have your thighs and ankles pressing against the pads. Fasten the seat belt. Loosely grasp the side handles.

Smoothly bring your legs together by pressing against the pads keeping your lower back pressed into the support. Hold this closed position momentarily, then control the movement back to the starting position. As the weights touch, repeat.

Concentrate on the inner thighs doing the movement, not the lower leg.

Breathe easily throughout the exercise.

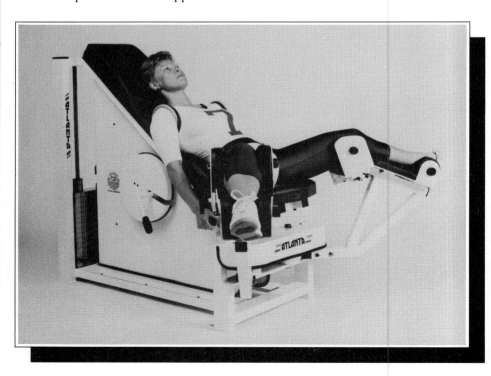

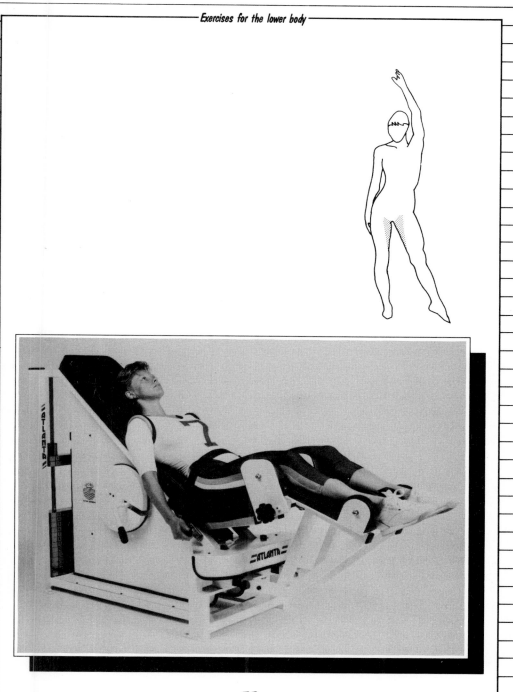

Hip abduction machine
For the muscles of the outer hip and thigh

Place the selector pin in the right position in the weight stack for you. Adjust the lever on the side of the machine so that the movement arms are together. Sit into the machine pressing your back firmly into the support. Place your legs in to the movement arms, with your thighs and ankles pressing against the pads. Fasten the seat belt. Loosely grasp the side handles.

Keeping your lower back pressed into the support, press the movement arms apart as wide as possible, then hold this position momentarily, before controlling the movement back to the starting position. As the arms touch, repeat.

Breathe easily throughout.

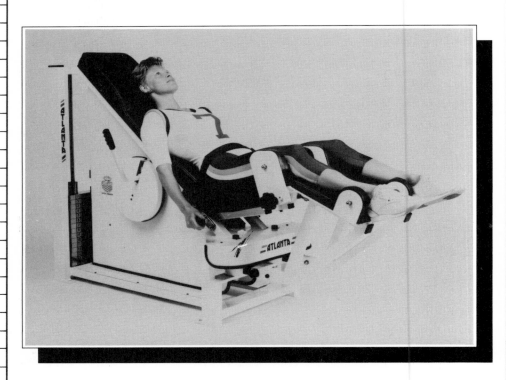

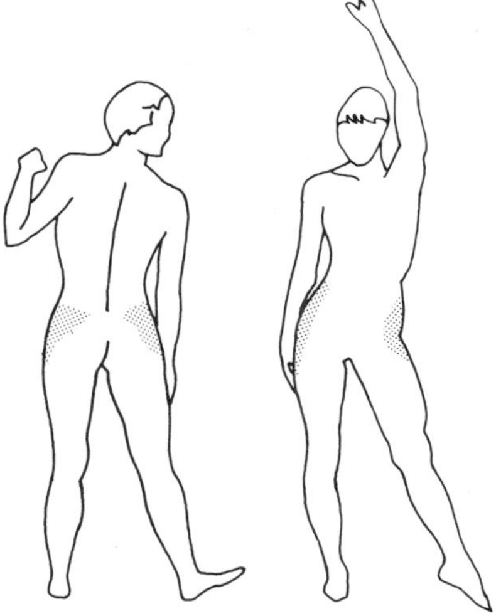

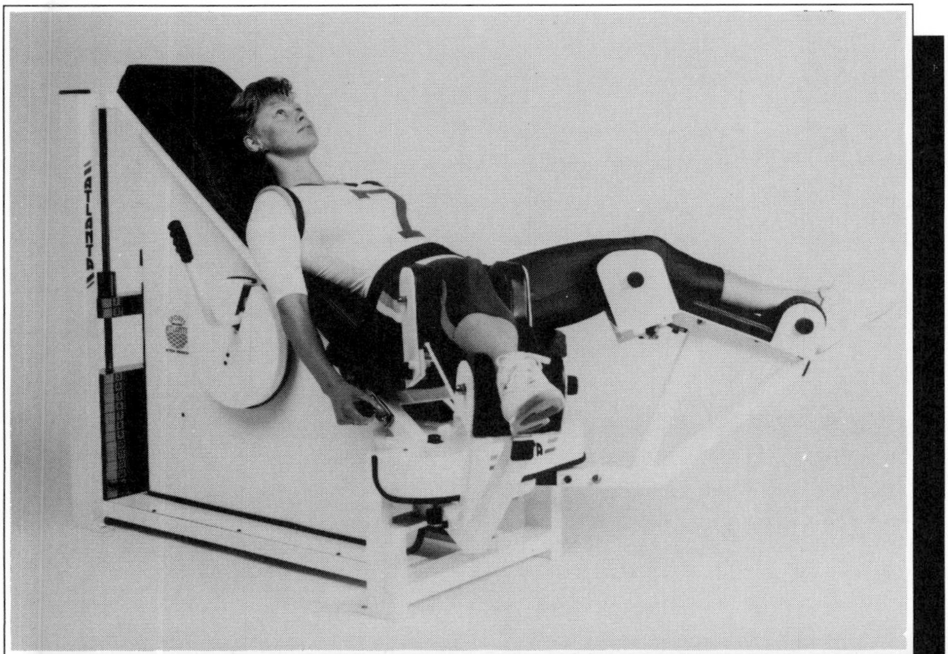
ATLANTA

Duo-symmetric squat machine

For the muscles of the buttocks, thighs and calves.

Place the selector pin in the right position in the weight stack for you. Adjust the seat using the side handle so that when you are positioned as illustrated, the angle at your knees is approximately 90 degrees. Your feet should be on the footplates with your shoulders firmly against the shoulder pads, lower back pressed into the support, head relaxed, with hands loosely clasped around the hand grips.

Push both legs away from you, breathing out as you do so. When you have reached full extension, but just before your knees lock, control the movement back to the starting position, breathing in just as the weights are about to touch the rest of the weight stack. Repeat.

This machine can be used to exercise one leg at a time, since there is a footplate for each leg. Carry out the instructions as above, but with one leg, then repeat on the other leg.

If there is no calf machine in the gym or health club, a squat machine, or leg press machine can be used very effectively to condition the muscles of the calves. In this case, extend your legs by fully straightening the knees and whilst maintaining this position, point your toes so that your heels come away from the footplates. Control the movement of your heels back to the footplate, then repeat.

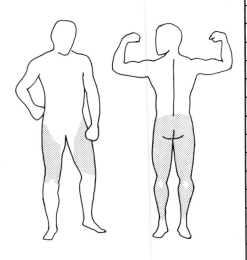

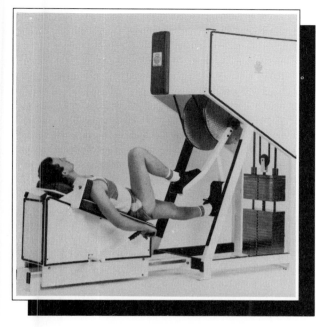

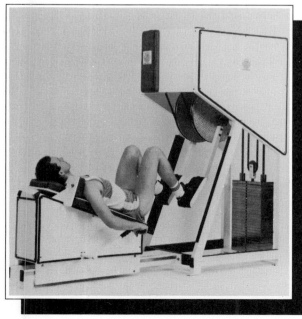

11
Exercises for the upper body

CHEST

Press on bench (Chest press)
For the muscles of the chest, back of upper arm and front of shoulder.

Lie with your back flat on a bench, making sure that your low back is pressed comfortably into the bench. You should maintain this position throughout the exercise.

Hold a barbell in this position at arms length with a fairly wide grip. You will need the help of a partner for this.

Smoothly lower the bar so that it touches the middle of your chest then press it upwards to arms length again. Repeat the sequence.

Breathe out as you raise the bar, and in as you lower it.

If an incline bench is used, it is possible to work the muscles of the chest in different ways. The higher the incline, the more the front of shoulder muscles are worked, and vice versa.

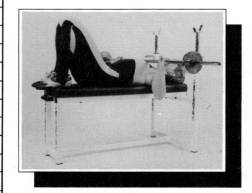

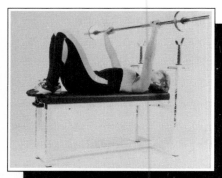

Dumb-bell flyes
For the muscles of the chest and front of shoulders.

Lie on a bench as in the previous exercise. This time hold a dumb-bell in each hand palms facing each other. Have your arms bent slightly at the elbow. The dumb-bells should be positioned above your chest.

From this position take the arms out to the side under control as far as possible, then smoothly return to the starting position.

Breathe in as you lower your arms and out as you raise them.

Seated decline bench press machine

For the muscles of the chest, front of shoulder, and back of the upper arm.

Place the selector pin in the right position in the weight stack for you. Adjust the seat height using the handle provided so that hands, shoulders and elbows are in the same line. Sit comfortably on the machine with your low back pressed into the support. Place your feet on the foot pedal and push it away from you — this will bring the movement arms into a forward position. Take the weight, maintaining a firm grip with wrists straight then take your feet from the foot pedal. Push the arms away from you smoothly, breathing out in the process. Go to full extension without locking your elbows, then control the movement back to the starting position, breathing in as you do so. As the weights touch the rest of the block, repeat.

When you have finished the required number of repetitions, place your feet back on the foot pedal and push it away from you. This will take the weight. Remove your arms from their position and return the weights using the footpedal.

Remember not to arch your back, keep your elbows high.

This exercise can be carried out with both narrow and wide grip.

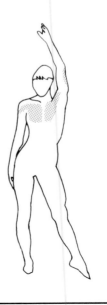

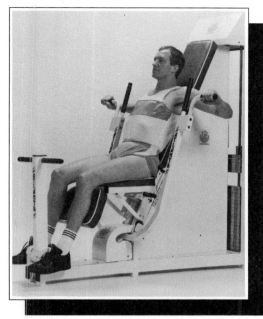

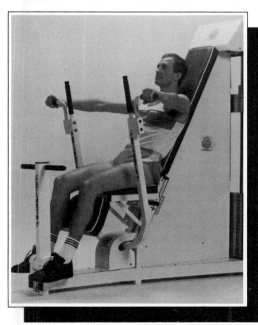

Vertical chest machine (pec deck)
For the muscles of the chest and front of shoulders.

Place the selector pin in the right position in the weight stack for you. Sit into the machine, making sure that your head, shoulders, lower back and buttocks are pressed into the rear pad. Place your forearms behind the pads of the movement arms so that your elbows are in line with your shoulders. Bring the movement arms together by pressing with your forearms against the pads, breathing out as you do so. Hold the pads together for a moment, then control the movement back to the starting position, breathing in just as the weights touch the rest of the block. Repeat.

This machine can also be used to work one side of the chest and shoulder at a time by using one arm only.

Note: it is often easier to enter the machine by first seating yourself, bringing one movement arm forward, then turning slightly to reach the other movement arm.

There is also a decline version of this machine which works the upper chest and front of shoulder muscles more. Instructions are similar.

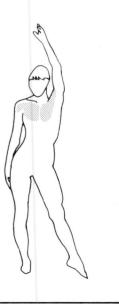

ARMS

Arm curl
For muscles of the front of the upper arm.

Stand tall, feet shoulder width apart. Grip a barbell with palms facing forward, hands slightly wider than hip width apart. Keeping your upright position, with upper arms remaining close to the sides of the body, bend your arms at the elbow, smoothly bringing the bar to meet the chest. Note that the upper arm remains in its fixed starting position and the movement takes place solely about the elbow joint. Smoothly return the bar to the starting position and repeat. Make sure you work through the full range of movement and avoid the tendency to lean forward or backward when lifting and lowering the bar.

Breathe in as you raise the bar and out as you lower it.

Alternate dumb-bell curl
For the muscles at the front of the upper arm.

The starting position is the same as for the previous exercise except that you are holding a dumb-bell in either hand, palms facing your sides, at arms length. Keeping the upper arm close to the body and standing tall throughout, bend one arm at the elbow to bring the dumb-bell to your shoulder, twisting the dumb-bell through ninety degrees as you do so. Smoothly return this dumb-bell to its starting position and repeat on the other side. As before, breathe in as you raise each weight and out as you lower.

Seated tricep press
For the muscles at the back of the upper arm.

Sit upright on a bench or sturdy chair. Place your feet apart and flat on the floor to give a firm stable base.

Hold a dumb-bell in one hand with the upper arm vertical, close to the head and flexed at the elbow.

Smoothly straighten this arm at the elbow, keeping the upper arm in exactly the same position in all times, then control the movement back to the starting position. Repeat the sequence on both sides.

Breathe in as you raise the weight and out as you lower it.

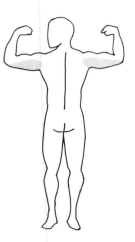

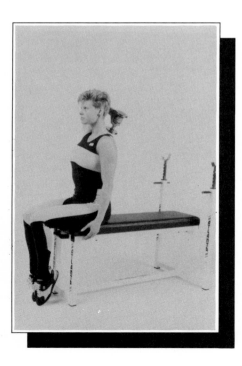

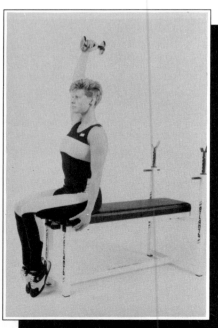

Multi exercise machine

Virtually all muscle groups can be worked using this machine since the number of exercises which can be carried out using it are limited only by your imagination.

Obvious exercises which can be done:

Pull-ups

For the muscles of the upper back and front of upper arm, as well as the forearm.

Grip the bar firmly with an under or overgrasp and hang at full stretch — tall people may find that they have to bend their legs slightly.

From this long hanging position, smoothly pull yourself up so that your head comes past the bar, breathing in as you do so. Hold this top position for a moment, then return smoothly and under control to your starting position, breathing out. Repeat.

For variety and to work the same muscles slightly differently, experiment with different grip widths.

The pull ups can be made progressively more difficult on this machine by using the weight belt attached to the weight stack.

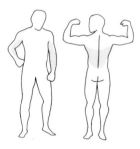

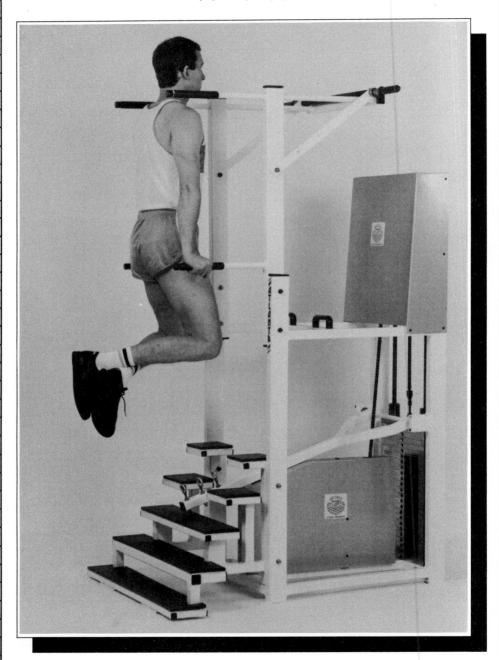

Dips

For the muscles of the upper back and shoulder and back of the upper arm.

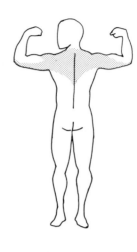

Position yourself so that you are supporting your weight on outstretched arms as in the illustration at left. Bend your knees slightly, but keep the rest of your body in a straight line. Now bend at the elbows so that you are lowering your body under control to a position where your elbows are at an angle of approximately 90°, breathing in as you do so. Keep your spine long.

From this position strongly push yourself back up to the starting position, and breathe out. Repeat.

As with the pull-ups exercise, the dips can be made progressively harder by using the weight belt and the weight stack as illustrated in the third picture.

Multi bicep machine
For the muscles at the front of the upper arm.

Place the selector pin in the right position in the weight stack for you. Adjust the seat (handle underneath the seat) so that when you are seated your shoulders are level with the pads. Position your elbows so that your elbows are opposite the point of rotation of the lever arms. Grip the handles firmly and pull these handles towards you by bending at the elbows breathing in as you do so. Make this a smooth controlled movement. Hold your top most position for a moment, then slowly lower the lever arms back to the starting position breathing out. Just as the weights touch the rest of the block, repeat.

Make sure that you do not arch your back.

This, and similar machines can be used to exercise one arm at a time.

Multi tricep machine
For the muscles at the back of the upper arm.

Place the selector pin in the right position in the weight stack for you. Adjust the seat (handle underneath the seat) so that when you are seated your shoulders are level with the pads. The machine is best entered by pushing one of the movement arms forward. Place your elbows in line with the point of rotation of the movement arms, with the sides of your hands on the hand pads, palms facing in.

Now straighten both arms by pressing against the hand pads, but make sure that your elbows remain on the front pad, still in line with the axis of rotation. Do not arch your spine.

Hold the fully straightened position for a moment, then slowly control the movement back to the starting position. Just as the weights touch the rest of the block, repeat.

Breathe out as you straighten, in as you return.

This machine can also be used to exercise one arm at a time, in alternate fashion.

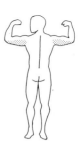

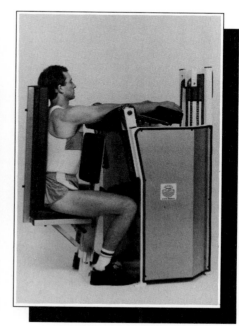

SHOULDERS

Seated press behind neck

For the muscles of the shoulders, backs of upper arms, upper back.

Place a bar or light barbell across your shoulders as for the half squat exercise, or get a partner to help you. Then sit upright on a bench or sturdy chair. Smoothly press the barbell upward so it ends up at arms length overhead. Return the barbell under control until it just touches the neck then repeat the sequence. Breathe in as you press the bar upward, and breathe out on the return movement.

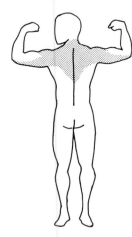

Seated alternate dumb-bell press

*For the muscles of the shoulders, backs of the
upper arms, and upper back.*

Sit upright on a bench or sturdy chair, with
a dumb-bell in each hand, palms facing
in at shoulder level. Smoothly press on
dumb-bell, upward and overhead to arms
length, then control its movement back
to the starting position before repeating
with the other arm.

Breathe in as you raise each arm, and out
as you lower.

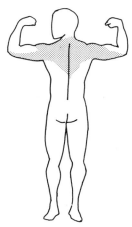

Upright rowing
For the muscles of the shoulders upper back and biceps.

Stand tall holding a barbell, palms facing your body with your hands spaced approximately two thumbs distance apart, with the bar at arms length in front of your body.

From this position pull the bar upward to neck height making sure you keep your elbows high throughout. Lower the bar to the starting position under control and repeat the sequence.

Make sure the bar travels in a straight line as close as possible to your body.

Breathe in as you raise the bar, and out as you lower it.

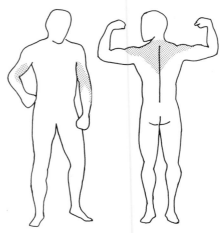

Standing side (lateral) raise

For the muscles of the shoulders and upper back.

Assume an upright posture with feet approximately hip width apart. Hold a dumb-bell in either hand, palms facing each other, just in front of the body, arms slightly bent at the elbows.

From this position, raise the dumb-bells simultaneously to the side to reach a position just above head height, then lower under control to the starting position and repeat.

Avoid the tendency to throw the weights upward or lean forwards or backwards.

Breathe in as you raise your arms and out as you lower them.

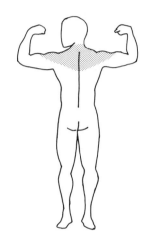

BACK

Single arm rowing

For the muscles of the upper back and front of upper arm.

Start with your feet comfortably apart, or with one knee on a bench bending forward from the waist using one hand to support yourself on the bench. Hold a dumb-bell at arms length in the other hand so that it is directly beneath the shoulder.

Smoothly bring the dumb-bell up to the side of the chest and then control the movement back to the starting position. Repeat on both sides. Make sure to keep your back flat throughout.

Breathe in as you lift the dumb-bell up, and out as you return it.

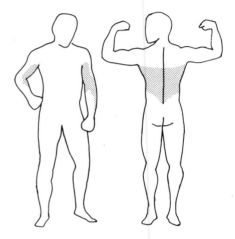

Hyperextensions
For the muscles of the back, the buttocks and the backs of the thighs.

Lie face down on a mat, with your hands either behind your head, or resting on the small of your back.

Whilst trying to keep the spine long, raise your chest off the floor, breathing in as you do so. Hold your uppermost position momentarily, then return to your starting position, breathing out in the process.

Many equipment manufacturers now make a special device for carrying out this exercise.

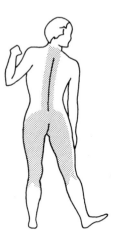

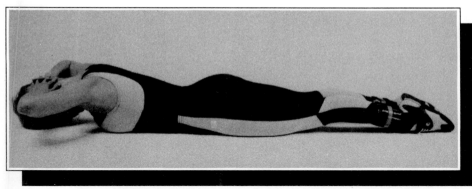

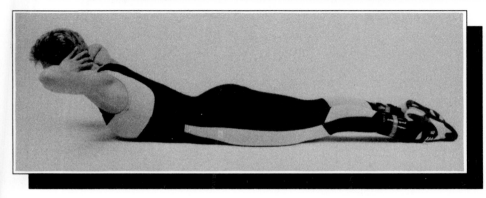

Pullover machine
For the muscles of the upper back and torso.

Place the selector pin in the right position in the weight stack for you. Adjust the seat (handle underneath) so that when you are seated your shoulders are in line with the point of rotation of the movement arm. When seated make sure that your back is pressed firmly into the support and the lap strap is fastened.

Press the foot pedal down so that the movement arm comes forward over your head, then place your arms so that your elbows are pressing against the pads and your hands are resting lightly on the back support bar. Allow your arms to go back over your head then take your feet from the foot pedal as you take the weight.

From this position bring your arms forward by pressing with your elbows against the pads until the support bar touches your lower abdomen. Hold this position for a moment, then control the movement back to your start position and repeat. When you have completed the desired number of repetitions, press down the foot pedal, which brings the movement arm forward and remove your arms.

Breathe out as you bring the support arm to your abdomen, and breathe in on the return.

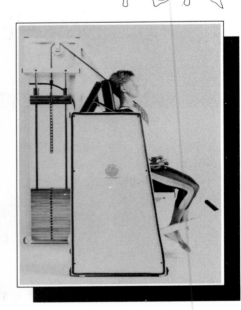

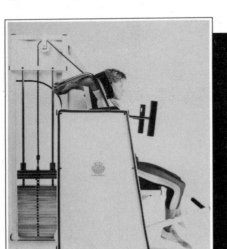

Rowing machine

For the muscles of the upper back and rear of the shoulder.

Place the selector pin in the right position in the weight stack for you. Sit on the machine with head, shoulders, lower back and buttocks pressed into the rear pad. Slide your arms through the roller pads so that the backs of your elbows are against the rollers. Press your elbows against the pads so that they move as far back as they will go, making sure that your elbows are at the same level as your shoulders. Hold this furthermost position for a moment, then control the movement back to the starting position. Just as the weight touches the rest of the block, repeat.

Keep your back straight at all times and do not jerk this movement. Breathe in as you press your elbows back and out on their return.

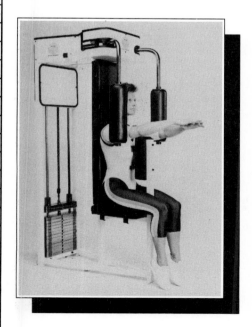

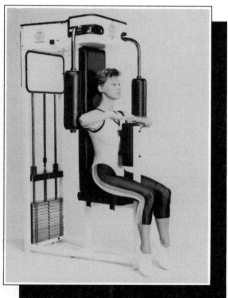

Torso arm machine (pulldown)

For the muscles of the upper back and front of the upper arm.

Place the selector pin in the right position in the weight stack for you. Adjust the seat height so that when seated you can just reach and grip firmly the handle or bar. Fasten the seat belt.

Gripping the handle pull bar to the front of the neck, keeping your elbows back and to the side, breathing out as you do so. Hold this position for a moment, then return to the starting position smoothly, breathing in. Repeat.

The bar can also be brought to the back of the neck, working the same muscles slightly differently.

If a wide bar is used, different grip widths can be experimented with.

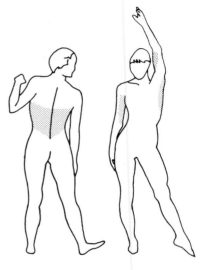

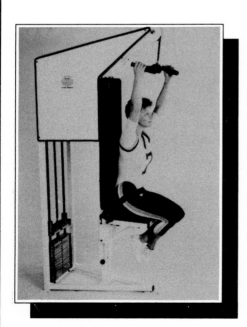

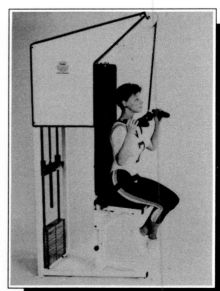

ABDOMINALS

To fully condition the abdominal muscles requires that you work in a number of different directions. One of the core exercises for abdominals in general is the curl up, lying on the floor.

Curl up

Lie flat on the floor, with your knees bent at an angle, feet flat on the floor, low back pressed into the ground, arms by sides. This is the basic position you should start all abdominal work from. Breathe in. As you breathe out slowly and in a controlled manner raise your head and shoulders off the floor. Your back must be rounded throughout. The better the condition of your abdominal muscles the more of your body you will be able to peel off the floor, yet there is no great advantage to be gained by coming up any higher than the position illustrated.

Hold your final position momentarily, then slowly curl down and repeat the sequence. Never allow your back to arch.

The exercise can be made more difficult by placing your hands across your chest and proceeding as before. The exercise is still more difficult with your hands behind your head.

Diagonal curl up

To work the diagonal muscles of the
abdomen. Assume the basic curl up
position, but come up with a twisting,
curling up movement. Do this by placing
one arm across the body and raising the
shoulder of this arm just as in the
illustration. Repeat the sequence on both
sides, breathing as before. This exercise
can also be made more difficult by placing
the arms folded across the chest or behind
the head. There are many variations in
abdominal exercises yet the basic rules
outlined must be followed.

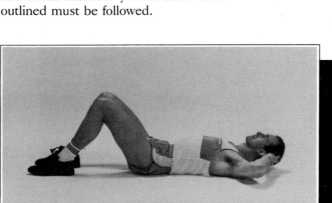

Alternate knee to elbow

Lie flat hands behind head, low back pressed into floor, knees slightly bent. Breathe in. As you breathe out, curl up, twisting as you do so to bring your left elbow to your right knee. Curl down and repeat on the other side.

Abdominal crunch

Lie on floor with your legs supported on a chair or bench. Your knees should be above your hips and your hands behind your head. Breathe in. As you breathe out curl your head and shoulders towards your knees. Hold momentarily then return to the starting position, still keeping your low back pressed into the floor.

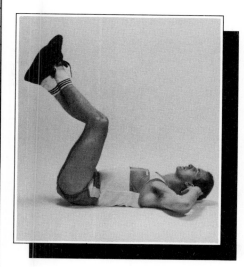

All the graded curl ups (straight up and on the diagonal) can also be advanced and carried out on an incline bench.

Do not go on to the incline until you can master the floor work.

U sit

Assume the position as illustrated. Breathe in. As you breathe out, raise your hips and shoulders off the floor at the same time. Hold the topmost position momentarily, then return to your starting position.

Abdominal machine

For the muscles at the front of the abdomen.

Place the selector pin in the right position in the weight stack for you. Adjust the seat height (handle underneath the seat) so that when you are seated, the lower part of your breastbone is opposite the axis of rotation. In the seated position, place your ankles behind the rollers, knees spread. Grip the handles above your head loosely and press your lower back firmly into the back support. Breathe in. As you breathe out, bring your ribs to your hips by contracting the abdominal muscles only — resist the temptation to pull with your arms and try to keep your legs relaxed. Hold your most contracted position for a moment, then return to your starting position, breathing in as you do so. As the weights touch, repeat. Keep your back pressed into the support at all times.

It is often useful for beginners to practise the basic curl ups before using this machine to get used to the feeling of isolating the abdominal muscles.

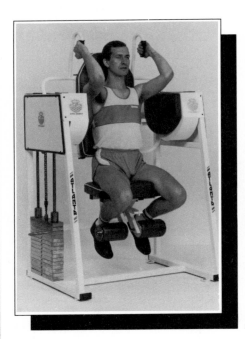

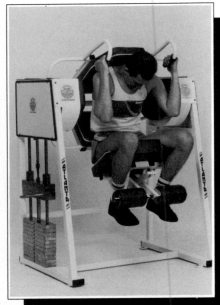

12

Warming down

When you have completed your weight training or activity session, your body will recover more quickly if you gradually bring it back to normal with exercise of decreasing intensity.

Light cycling on an exercise bicycle is a good idea, as is a gentle jog, followed by some of the general mobilizing work from the warm up section, such as the arm and shoulder circles, the legs swings, hip circles etc.

Because you are now warm, make use of this fact by engaging in some stretching work. Hold each stretch position for about 30 seconds and repeat twice to begin with. The time spent stretching can be increased if you feel that you are particularly inflexible.

Remember: Do not stop still particularly after strenuous exercise, and avoid the temptation to sit down immediately. If you do stop or sit down, all the blood which has been directed to working muscles will find it very difficult to get back to the heart. This 'pooling' of the blood in the extremities can leave you feeling light-headed and nauseous, and you may even faint. Keeping your muscles working with light regular activity will improve your recovery and the muscles will act as little pumps forcing the blood back to the heart.

Calf stretch (gastrocnemius)

Stand at an incline to a wall or barre resting your weight on your hands opposite your shoulders as in the illustration. Place one leg forward, with the knee over the toe, with the other leg stretched out behind you, heel pressed into the floor. Your hips should face the wall at all times and your feet should remain hip distance apart. Gradually inch back your rear foot, still keeping the heel on the floor until you feel a stretch in the back calf. Hold this position for a few seconds, then release. Repeat 6 times for each leg, breathing easily throughout.

Calf stretch (soleus)

Position as for the previous exercise, but bend the knee of the back leg slightly, still keeping the heel pressed into the floor. You will feel the stretch lower down in the calf. Repeat and breathe as for the previous exercise.

Hamstrings (seated)

Sit comfortably on a mat placed on the floor, making sure that you are sitting with spine lengthened and perched on your 'sitting bones'. Your legs should be fully stretched out in front of you with your knees pressed into the floor. From this position, hinge forward from the hips, so that your upper body moves forward as a unit. Some people may find that they do not move very far at all but move as far as you can whilst keeping your spine long, breathing easily throughout and holding your furthermost position for 30 seconds. If the stretch subsides at all, move forward a little more, then release by bending your knees.

Repeat the exercise this time with legs fully extended as before, but with spine rounded. Aim to get your head closer to your knees. Again hold your furthermost position moving closer to your knees as the stretch subsides.

The illustrations show the exercises with feet flexed — for variety, experiment with the toes pointed.

Remember to breathe through the stretches.

Buttocks and hip flexors of opposite leg

From a lying down position on a mat, bring one leg up to your chest and hold it there in place with your hands clasped around the knee. Have the opposite leg stretched out along the floor, foot flexed, knee pressed into the floor. Keep your low back pressed into the floor also by pulling your tummy in. Hold this position for 30 seconds, breathing easily throughout the exercise, bringing your knee closer into your chest only if your outstretched leg and lower back remain in their stretched and flattened positions respectively.

Repeat on the other side.

Groin and inner thigh

Still in the lying position adopted for the previous exercise, bring both feet together and allow your knees to fall out to the side. Again make sure that your lower back is still pressed into the floor. Experiment with the position of your feet and knees relative to your buttocks to see where you get the most stretch in your groin, then hold this position for 30 seconds, breathing easily through the exercise.

Spine and outer thigh

From an upright seated position with your legs stretched out in front of you, place one foot to the outside of your outstretched leg. Make sure that your back is long. Now turn so that the opposite arm can push against the knee of the crossed leg and try and turn your upper body round so that your shoulders are facing to the side and you are looking over one shoulder. Do not allow the shoulders to lift up and do not fall back but keep the spine long and rotated. Hold your furthermost position, breathing through the stretch, for 30 seconds. Repeat on the other side.

Hamstrings and inner thigh

From an upright and seated position on the floor, keep one leg fully outstretched, foot flexed, knee pressed into the floor, and bring the other leg in bent at the knees so that the heel of the foot rests up in the groin, knee as close to the floor as possible. Hold your back as upright as possible, then try and hinge forward from the hips as in the first stretch, still keeping the spine long. Hold your furthermost position for 30 seconds, then release by rounding your back and bringing your head to your outstretched knee.

Repeat on the other side.

Spine and front of trunk

Lie face down on a mat with your hands approximately at shoulder level. Keeping your spine long and your head in alignment press against the floor and slowly straighten your arms so that your back arches. Make sure that your hips remain in contact with the floor. Breathe throughout the stretch, holding your topmost position for 30 seconds.

Release by rolling over on to your back and hugging your knees into your chest.

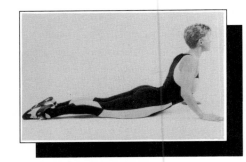

Front of thigh (Quad)

Stand upright with good posture, with one hand resting on a chair back or barre for balance. Clasp the foot of your outside leg in one hand and bring it close to your buttocks, yet still keeping the knee of this leg in the same position opposite the knee of the supporting leg, and without arching the spine.

Hold this furthermost position for 30 seconds, release and repeat on the other side.

Front of chest

Repeat the shoulder squeeze exercise as described in the warm up section (page 52), but hold the furthermost position for 30 seconds before releasing.

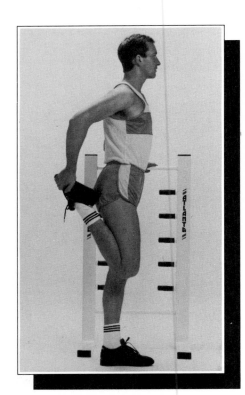

Upper back

From a tall standing position, interlock your fingers and hold your arms outstretched at shoulder level. Tilt your pelvis so that your bottom tucks under — you may have to bend your knees slightly. From this position, try to push your hands further away from you and hold the furthermost position for 30 seconds, breathing easily through the stretch.

Side trunk

Repeat the side bend exercise as described in the warm up section (page 53) but extend one arm over the head to make the exercise stronger. Hold your furthermost position for 30 seconds, breathing easily through the stretch.

13

Nutrition and exercise

What you eat is going to influence how you feel and how you exercise too. This book makes no claims to be a diet book, but the following guidelines should help you maximise your training as well as helping you to live a healthier life.

EVERYDAY DIET

Many authorities now blame the food we eat for many health problems ranging from high blood-pressure and obesity to skin complaints and allergies.

A good general diet should include plenty of fresh vegetables and fruit, a good quantity of cereals (wholemeal pastas, muesli, whole grains, etc) and a variety of beans and pulses.

Meat intake should emphasize white meats such as chicken and turkey, as well as white fish rather than red meats which tend to hide large quantities of saturated fat.

Avoid high fat foods such as pies and pastries, sausages and salamis and go easy on salad dressings such as mayonnaise.

Cut down on confectionery and sweets, as well as watching your alcohol intake — all those extra and empty calories will re-appear as fat on your body!

Take plenty of fluids in the form of water as well as fresh fruit juices, and cut down on your tea and coffee intake.

Switch to skimmed or semi-skimmed milk.

Trim off visible fat from any meats you eat, and grill rather than fry.

Steam vegetables to keep them at their most nutritious.

Cut down on the use of butter.

Cut out salt added to food.

Eat at regular intervals throughout the day, rather than cramming all your food in at one go. Try not to leave your main meal until the last thing in the evening. Smaller more frequent meals are preferable.

Snack on fruit or raw vegetables.

Indulge yourself every now and again!

Vitamin supplements or not?

Many people feel that they should take extra vitamins or minerals if they are training hard. Some would argue that a well-balanced diet includes all the necessary vitamins and supplements you are likely to need, even in heavy training, and that supplements are a waste of time since very often they are not in the form that the body can easily accept and often end up enriching the sewers and lightening your pocket. Other people, and many professional sportsmen, swear that they need extra vitamins or minerals and that they feel much better for taking them.

If you are not getting an adequate diet then you may indeed be lacking certain vitamins and minerals — this may also be the case if you are training very hard indeed. Average people following the guidelines given and exercising as recommended in this text should not have a problem.

Does muscle building require a high meat intake?

For a long time anybody who wanted to put on muscle mass was recommended to eat lots of meat. This is now known as being useless advice. Heavy training such as you would carry out for muscle building requires more than anything that you have lots of carbohydrate in your diet. This is because the muscles can store carbohydrate as glycogen for subsequent heavy exercise. Having done the exercise the glycogen stores are depleted and must be replenished. If you are engaged in heavy exercise or training eat more carbohydrates such as wholemeal bread, pastas, grains, cereals, etc.

Start replenishing with carbohydrates as soon after your exercise bout as possible, along with replacing lost fluids.

Generally speaking you need to consume about 1000 Kcals a day above your normal daily requirements to provide the energy for the heavy training necessary for an increase in muscle mass. This is a guideline only, and although you will need to consume more calories, make sure you are not consuming more than you need and thereby increasing your body fat percentage. Watch and monitor this if possible by skinfold measurements.

Exercise and weight loss

It is possible to control your weight very effectively through exercise. The best type of exercise for using up body fat is that which is of low intensity, and long duration.

If you have only a few pounds of fat to get rid of, then provided you keep your diet the same in terms of calories consumed and you increase the number of calories you expend through exercise, then there is no need to diet. However you may not lose weight as such, since the extra exercise may build muscle tissue as well as burn up fat, leaving your body weight the same although you will look and feel completely different.

If you have a lot of weight to lose, then a combination of diet and exercise is the answer. Do not attempt to restrict your calorie intake too much however: you should aim with your exercise and diet to lose only one or two pounds per week. Because this is such a difficult area, it is best to consult more specialist advice from an exercise specialist/physiologist, or read some of the many detailed books on the subject which are now available (see recommended reading list).

Appendix 1

INJURIES

For all but the simplest problems you should get specialist advice. An injury which does not get the right treatment is liable to give you recurring trouble. Some points to remember:

1. Do not continue exercising on an injury. Stop what you are doing. Treat any swelling with ice (wrapped in a towel, or plastic bag if no ice pack is available. Frozen goods, like a bag of peas will suffice in an emergency).

2. Bandage an injured limb and place it on a pillow in a slightly elevated position.

3. Pain of inflammation can usually be relieved by aspirin.

4. A sprain is an injury to a joint and often involves damage to the ligaments of that joint to a greater or lesser degree.

5. A strain is an injury to a muscle or tendon.

6. Both strains and sprains are categorized by degree. First degree indicates that the injury is minor and will be accompanied by tenderness, some swelling and pain. Second degree injuries involve more damage with much greater tenderness, pain and swelling. Third degree injuries invariably involve complete tears in connective tissues and will need specialist treatment.

7. Delayed onset muscle soreness and general stiffness, whilst not an injury as such, can be troublesome. Both complaints are an indication of doing too much exercise of too great an intensity, too soon. Both conditions can best be treated by thoroughly warming the muscles and joints involved (a warm bath is ideal) then carrying out some light stretching whilst dressed in warm clothing.

8. Stitch in the side. Again not an injury, but irritating and alarming if you have not experienced it before. Due often to a lack of oxygen and blood flow to certain muscles, the problem can be relieved by breathing deeply, whilst decreasing the intensity of your exercise slightly.

9. Cramp. Another indication that muscles have been working hard, or that you are not getting enough fluid in your diet, or both. Immediate treatment to relieve the 'knotting' of the muscle is to stretch out the affected muscle. Always replace lost fluids, especially if you sweat heavily following exercise, or if the exercise is prolonged, during the activity at frequent intervals.

Appendix 2

TRAINING ZONE — HEART RATE METHOD

One way which is being used increasingly to determine whether you are working hard enough, or too hard, whilst you are exercising, is to use your heart rate as a guide to exercise intensity or against over-exertion. As you do more work or exercise, your body will demand more blood to be supplied to working muscles to supply them with oxygen and nutrients and remove carbon dioxide and disperse other products. Because of this, your heart will have to increase its rate of beating to cope with the new demand.

As a general guide, the *maximum* rate of beating of the human heart is obtained by taking your age in years away from the number 220. The figure you are left with is your maximum heart rate. Your *resting* heart rate is best taken before you have done any work or exercise at all, such as first thing in the morning when you have just woken up.

If you take your resting value from your age adjusted maximum, this will give you your heart rate *reserve* figure.

To find your training zone, multiply the heart rate reserve figure by 0.7 and 0.9 respectively and add the figure you get in each case to your resting heart rate. This gives you the lower and upper end of your aerobic training zone. Beginners should stay at the lower end of the training zone for several weeks until their fitness begins to improve, when it will then be safe to work at slightly higher levels if necessary. There is no advantage to be gained by working at much greater intensity than your maximum as given by this method, in terms of improving aerobic fitness.

Example:

A 30-year-old man with a resting heart rate of 60 beats per minute.

$220 - 30 = 190$ (Maximum age adjusted heart rate)

$190 - 60 = 130$ (Heart rate reserve)

$130 \times 0.7 = 91$

$91 + 60 = 151$ (Training Heart rate — lower end of zone)

$130 \times 0.9 = 117$

$117 + 60 = 177$ (Training heart rate — upper end of zone)

To take your pulse rate

Find your radial artery by lightly pressing your fingers to the inside of your wrist (see diagram overleaf). Once you have located the pulse, count the number of times your heart beats in 10 seconds. Multiply this figure by 6 in order to get your heart rate in beats per minute.

Taking your pulse rate is a useful guide to exercise intensity only if the exercise in question is fairly sustained in its nature. As a guide to the intensity of exercise

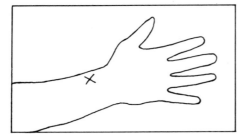 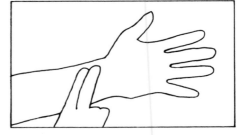

whilst you are weight training it is not so good, since in maintaining certain exercise positions, many muscles will have to contract statically thereby impeding blood flow. This in turn tends to give rise to an increase in blood-pressure which occurs often through an increase in the rate of beating of the heart. In such cases, the increased beating of the heart no longer reflects the demands of the working muscles as during continuous steady activity.

Remember too, that many things affect heart rate (mood, emotion, alcohol, temperature, caffeine, smoking, drugs, illness, etc) and you should bear this in mind if you are exercising under different circumstances.

Appendix 3

COMMON POSTURAL PROBLEMS AND HOW TO DEAL WITH THEM

As long as there are no medical grounds why you should not be exercising, then the following postural problems can be helped with the following exercises.

Lumbar lordosis   Basic curl up, p103
Diagonal curl up, p104

Rounded back   Abdominal Crunch, p105
Stretch (Quad), p116
Stretch, p117
Shoulder squeeze, p52
Pulldown (wide grip), p102

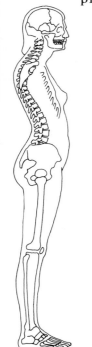

Lumbar lordosis

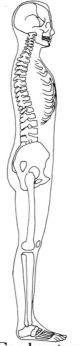

Good posture

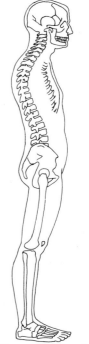

Rounded back

Appendix 4

CHOOSING A HEALTH CLUB OR GYMNASIUM

Your choice of exercise venue should reflect what you want out of it. You should make sure that it has everything which you are likely to need not only in terms of exercise equipment and facilities, but also in terms of showers, changing rooms, saunas, etc. Some clubs are very sociable places, and are always organizing events, have their own bar and restaurant, and are almost worth joining for their social side alone!

Make sure you get what you want by making a check list of what you think you need now, and what you think you might need in the future, then go and visit a few clubs near your home or workplace. Remember that if your exercise venue is too far away from either, is awkward to get to, or perhaps does not have convenient parking, your are less likely to exercise regularly.

All good clubs will give you a complimentary tour of their facilities, and many will insist on giving you a free exercise session or fitness test. Always take advantage of this, since it gives you the ideal opportunity to try the facilities, and get the feel of the place. Do not be pressurized into making your decision immediately — shop around your vicinity and weigh up the pros and cons of each venue before you part with your money.

If possible ask people who are members of a club what they feel about it, using their comments along with your observations and needs to finally make up your mind.

Compile a list of your needs like this. Visit several clubs in your area, checking them off against your requirements.

Ideal club:

Easily reached by own, or public transport.
Has a good sized, easy access car park.
Pleasant location.
Large gym with free weights, and single or multi station equipment.
Large space for warming up and stretching.
Has exercise bikes, treadmills and rowing machines for variety.
Knowledgeable and friendly staff.
Clean, airy and well ventilated.
Ambient atmosphere.
Not too crowded when I want to exercise.
Individually designed exercise programmes, featuring a fitness test at regular intervals.
Plenty of available lockers.
Clean changing rooms with showers.
Sauna and steam room.
Sunbeds.
Therapy rooms.
Other exercise classes.
Crèche.
Restaurant and bar.
Lots of social activities.

Appendix 5

WEIGHT TRAINING AT HOME

Some people prefer to exercise at home, rather than join a club or gum. If you think that weight training at home would be more convenient for you, bear in mind first what you will need in terms of space and equipment.

You will need a space which is large enough to do all your exercises in, and to store/position your equipment. Preferably this space should be well ventilated. Using free weights, you will need to cover the floor surface with a non slip mat, and the floor should be strong enough to take the total weight of you and your equipment. There also needs to be sufficient space overhead for any exercise involving upwardly stretched arms. In an ideal world, a separate room would be set aside as your home gym.

Choice of equipment will reflect what you want to do and how much money you have available. Absolute beginners will find that a lot can be achieved with a small dumb-bell/barbell kit and perhaps some strap on wrist and ankle weights. The smaller your weights set though, the harder it is to do some form of circuit training since you will not be able to have as many different bars set up for the different exercises you will be doing. Certain exercises will also require a bench or stands. Certain exercises you will not be able to do without more specialized home gynasiums which are now being marketed by several companies. If you go for one of these, ensure it is sturdy, easily adjustable and has enough weight — many come with pitifully small weight stacks which you have outgrown in a few weeks of regular exercise.

Home exercise bikes and rowing machines are still very popular, and if you are going for one of these to complement your weights workout, again make sure it is well made and sturdy, as well as being fully adjustable (saddle and handlebars) and can tell you how far and how fast you have gone, as well as how hard you are working.

Most beginners to exercise might find it easier to join a club before they decide upon a home gym. In so doing, they will find out exactly what they need.

Appendix 6

RECOMMENDED READING

Anatomy/kinesiology/biomechanics

G.J. Tortora & N.P. Anagnostakos, *Principles of Anatomy & Physiology* (4th ed) Harper & Row, 1984

K.F. Wells & K. Luttgens, *Kinesiology*, W.B. Saunders, 1976

R. Wirhed, *Athletic Ability & the Anatomy of Motion*, Wolfe Medical, 1984

Physiology/exercise physiology

D. Lamb, *Physiology of Exercise*, Macmillan, 1984

E.L. Fox & D.K. Matthews, *The Physiological Basis of Physical Education and Athletics*, Saunders, 1976

W.D. McArdle, F.I. Katch & V.L. Katch, *Exercise Physiology*, Lea & Febiger, 1981

A.C. Guyton, *Human Physiology & Mechanisms of Disease*, Saunders, 1982

Nutrition

F.I. Katch & W.D. McArdle, *Nutrition, Weight Control & Exercise*, Houghton Mifflin, 1977

Training

G. Schmolinsky, *Track and Field* Sportverlag Berlin, 1978

D. Harre, *Principles of Sports Training*, Sportverlag Berlin, 1982

E. Newsholme & T. Leech, *The Runner,* Fitness Books, 1983

D. L. Costill, *A Scientific Approach to Distance Running,* Track & Field News, 1979

K.H. Cooper, *The New Aerobics*, Bantam, 1970

General

R. Binney (Ed), *The BUPA Manual of Fitness & Wellbeing*, Macdonald & Co, 1984

R. J. Shephard, *Fitness and Health in Industry*, Karger, 1986

N. Clarke, *The Athlete's Kitchen*, CBI Publications, 1981

V. Grisogono, *Sports Injuries — A Self Help Guide*, John Murray, 1984

T. Moule, *Fit for Sport*, Patrick Stephens Ltd, 1986

Index

Of further interest . . .

Weight Training for Men
Weight Training for Women

Why bother with weights? Because by using weights you increase the load upon any given set of muscles thus INCREASING stamina and performance but DECREASING the time needed to achieve it. In these two books **Tony Lycholat** — a qualified British Amateur Weight Lifting Association teacher — shows how to use weights for maximum benefit. **WEIGHT TRAINING FOR MEN** shows how to improve stamina, firm-up muscles, build an outstanding physique and improve sports performance. **WEIGHT TRAINING FOR WOMEN** gives specific exercises for toning and trimming the figure — without building bulging muscles — and for retaining, or re-capturing, youthful health and beauty.

WEIGHT TRAINING FOR MEN

Tony Lycholat

WEIGHT TRAINING FOR WOMEN

Tony Lycholat